MILITARY MANUAL
OF
SELF-DEFENSE

MILITARY MANUAL
OF
SELF-DEFENSE

A COMPLETE GUIDE TO HAND-TO-HAND COMBAT

by
Anthony B. Herbert, Colonel, U.S. Army (Ret.)

HIPPOCRENE BOOKS
New York

HIPPOCRENE BOOKS
171 Madison Avenue
New York, N.Y. 10016

Library of Congress Cataloging in Publication Data

Herbert, Anthony B.
  Military manual of self-defense.

  1. Hand-to-hand fighting — Handbooks, manuals, etc.
I. Title.
U167.5.H3H47 1983   355.5'48   83-48633
ISBN 0-88254-708-9

Contents

Foreword

It would sadden me greatly to think that people who hear of this book will say that I am a violent man. Throughout my life, both in the Army and out, I have wished for and worked for a humane, just and reasoned world. There is no doubt that when I served this country as a soldier and officer I killed enemy soldiers and I would do so again if called upon to serve in battle. There is equally no doubt that I never killed or tortured civilians, women, children, unarmed enemy soldiers or prisoners of war. Moreover, I never condoned such acts and constantly struggled to prevent the commission and cover-up of such crimes. My efforts to prevent such crimes led to the ending of my Army career. I have always believed that such acts are intolerable and I will continue to speak out against them as long as I have breath to do so.

War involves killing, and those who say otherwise are unrealistic at best. No war, however, need involve more than killing the armed enemy who will otherwise kill you. We need to understand this and be prepared to defend ourselves if and when the need arises. I want this book to increase understanding of those survival needs and truths. And no more. Compassion, respect for life and human dignity and, above all, honor, must distinguish us if we are worthy of surviving. I trust and hope that we will prove to be worthy of survival.

It is presented to make accessible to all who care, what has previously been the property of only those who have so many times used such information and skills to our disadvantage — in order that good men may have an equal opportunity at survival.

Knowledge is neither good nor evil. It is truth. How it is utilized, for good or evil, is the responsibility of the user. This specific information can only be used, much like a surgeon's scalpel, to go after very special isolated targets. Let those who advocate the use of atomic, nuclear and neutron bombs look to themselves for what and who is good or evil. And let each look to his own judgments as revelations of what is his own character and personality.

Introduction

The text, simply stated, is a how-to cook book of individual hand-to-hand combat. Its purpose is to provide techniques and procedures of self-defense that require no extended practice or physical conditioning prior to practical application. Its premise is that hand-to-hand combat has but one purpose — to kill or disable an opponent. The ultimate aim of self-defense is survival.

The techniques explained will work. They will disable and/or kill an opponent. You will learn to defend yourself by disabling your attacker. If you jab the sharpened rattail end of a comb into your opponent's temple (as I suggest in the book) he will not become angrier and hurt you worse; he will probably die and he will certainly cease to be a threat.

No one is expected to learn all of the techniques explained in this volume, nor should you. Just select those few which will serve you and which you feel comfortable performing — AND ARE WILLING TO USE TO SAVE YOURS OR ANOTHER'S LIFE! Practice them a few times manually and more often mentally. And when they become necessary USE THEM.

The techniques in this text have been carefully selected in accordance with the following set of standards:

1. Their application is based upon minimum effort and therefore does not require strenuous physical preparation over a long period nor any particular warming up, stretching or limbering exercises prior to initiation.

2. They are the type of actions which can be applied under street and/or battlefield conditions while in normal street or battlefield attire.

3. Anyone can perform them. They are not based upon size, weight, age or gender.

4. They require a minimum of practice to learn and to maintain.

5. All techniques presented are devised so as to lead to inflicting maximum serious damage to any attacker, regardless of attacker's size or strength.

6. All techniques presented are for use in actual hand-to-hand defensive combat — AND ARE NEVER TO BE USED AS A PARTY GAME, SPORT, OR TO IMPRESS A FRIEND OR LOVER.

7. **They will work.**

General Principles of Defense

PREPARATION

1. THINK AHEAD AND BE PREPARED. Always keep in mind that the attacker is the one who will choose the time and the turf — and you're going to need every edge available.

2. NEVER LET YOUR GUARD DOWN. Remember, most victims are attacked in the vicinity or "safety" of their own residences.

3. STUDY YOUR ENVIRONMENT AND PLAN TO MAKE USE OF IT. No matter how familiar you are with the turf, practice the game of "what if I were attacked right now."

4. PREPARE A SET OF DEFENSIVE PLANS for every possible situation — and practice your moves over and over again.

5. ARM YOURSELF AS HEAVILY AS POSSIBLE under the circumstances — ALWAYS! Get a permit and carry a gun, if possible, or a knife, a kiyoga, a jawara stick, cane, umbrella or whatever *BUT GO ARMED, AND STAY ARMED, EVEN AT HOME.*

6. TREAT ALL ASSAILANTS AS DANGEROUS — regardless of age, size, sex or demeanor.

ATTACK

1. ATTACK FIRST. Aggressiveness wins — "waiting until" normally means "waiting until it's too late." Once you have determined action is inevitable, go for it first.

2. GO FOR BROKE. Once you decide to attack, don't hesitate or falter. Respond violently and maniacally; explode into action. Hit, chop, bite, kick, scream, gouge, tear or rip until your assailant is

out of it or dead. Remember, you may not get a second chance. *It is better to be tried by 12 than carried by 6.*

3. NEVER FIGHT ANYONE ON EQUAL TERMS — use rocks, bottles, dirt or sand to the eyes, jab with a ball point pen to the eyes, spray mace, swing a lead pipe or cue stick, bite, gouge out the eyes; be ruthless, deceptive, dirty; use your knife or any other weapon, even against an unarmed opponent. *SEEK THE ADVANTAGE ALWAYS – AND USE IT!*

4. FIGHT TO KILL (or disable) — go berserk; scream, yell, pinch, spit in the face, fight to destroy.

5. KEEP YOUR EYES ON YOUR ENEMY — never turn your back nor leave your feet intentionally.

6. ATTACK VITAL AND VULNERABLE AREAS of your opponent's body — the object is to destroy.

7. STAY ALERT AND DON'T PANIC — force yourself to think; that hype in your guts is adrenalin; it can help speed up reaction. *FORCE YOURSELF TO CONCENTRATE.*

8. END THE FIGHT AS RAPIDLY AS POSSIBLE — give no quarter; be totally ruthless; do not stop short of total victory.

9. LEAVE THE SCENE; don't hang around for kudos — MOVE OUT! And get a lawyer if you believe it may become necessary.

Some important things to remember about your assailant:

1. Never bad-mouth an assailant, nor threaten to get even later. It will accomplish nothing, and may provoke him to greater violence than anticipated.

2. Don't attempt to put him down or humiliate him. It may provoke him to put you down a little more than he originally intended, just to teach you a lesson.

3. If he talks, respond in as calm and steady a voice and manner as possible, *BUT DO NOT ATTEMPT TO STALL HIM OR REFER TO HIS IDEAS AS IDIOTIC.* This may enrage him to the point of no return.

4. Treat the encounter as serious, not as a trivial or matter-of-fact occurrence. Your assailant will want to prove that he is important and powerful.

5. NEVER BELIEVE AN ASSAILANT WHO ASSURES YOU HE IS ONLY AFTER YOUR CASH, AND ONLY WANTS TO TIE YOU UP "FOR A BIT". There's no need to go into a great explanation — just remember that Charles Manson convinced Sharon Tate and her guests, and one of them was a Karate expert, to be tied up. We know the result.
   When your assailant wants to tie you up, it's time to really consider a counter-attack. By either refusing and talking them out of it or by going for broke before you end up in an even more vulnerable position than you already are in.

6. Never offer money; if its money that's wanted, he'll ask for it. Many assailants look upon such an offer as an insult — the rich guy trying to use money as the muscle he doesn't have. Terrorists especially consider such an offer an insult to their personal esteem.

I   Unarmed Defense

1 Natural Weapons of the Body

THE WEAPONS:

The knuckles (**1**).

Edge of the hand (**2**).

Edge of the fist (**3**).

The fingers (**4**).

Heel of the hand (**5**).

The elbow (**6**).

The forearm (**7**).

The knee (**8**).

The foot (**9**).

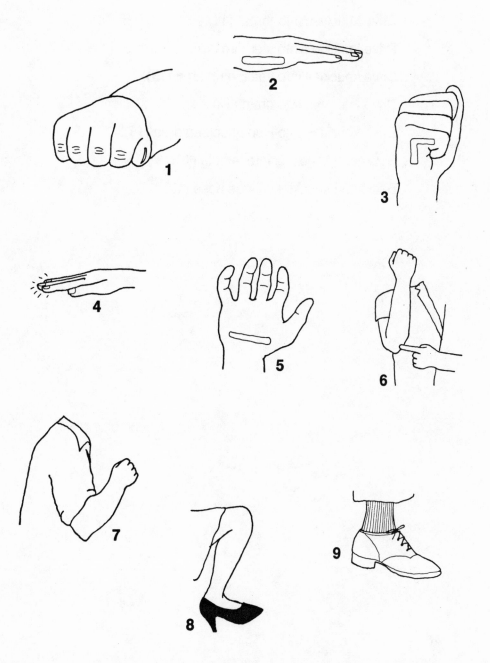

THE KNUCKLES — TO KILL:

Drive knuckles into temple (**10**).

Drive knuckles into throat (**11**).

Drive knuckles into sternum (**12**).

Drive knuckles into floating rib area (**13**).

Drive knuckles into groin (**14**).

Drive knuckles into kidney-spleen area (**15**).

Backhand knuckles into temple (**16**).

Backhand knuckles across nose (**17**).

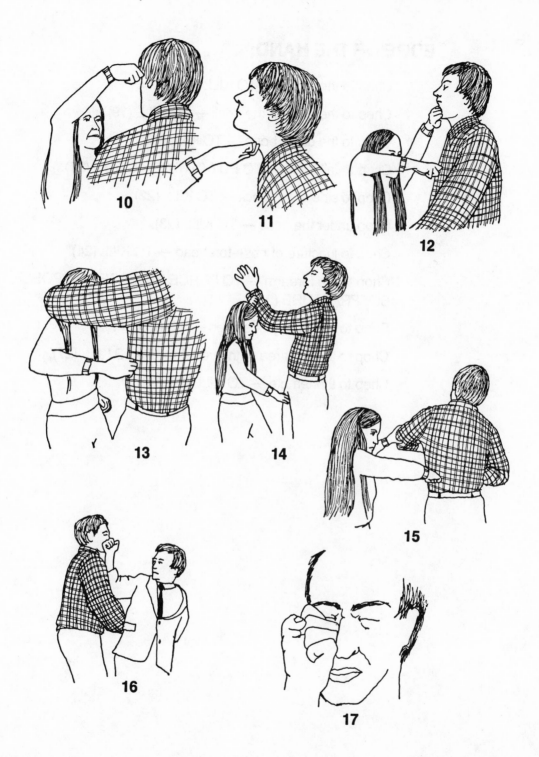

EDGE OF THE HAND:

Chop to the throat — TO KILL (**18**).

Chop to the back of the neck — TO KILL (**19**).

Chop to the collar bone — TO KILL (**20**).

Chop to tail bone — TO PUT OUT-OF-ACTION (**21**).

Chop to side of the neck — TO KILL (**22**).

Chop under the nose — TO KILL (**23**).

Chop to juncture of nose-forehead — TO KILL (**24**).

Chop to the forearm — TO FORCE RELEASE AND POSSIBLY FRACTURE (**25**).

Chop to the kidney or spleen — TO KILL (**26**).

Chop to the top area of the vertebrae — TO KILL (**27**).

Chop to the temple — TO KILL (**28**).

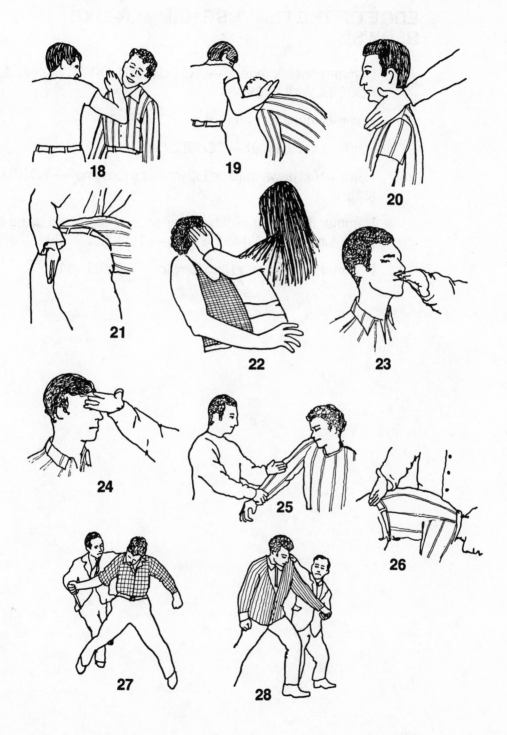

18

19

20

21

22

23

24

25

26

27

28

EDGE OF THE FIST (USE HAMMER-LIKE BLOWS):

Hammer nose-forehead — TO PUT OUT-OF-ACTION AND POSSIBLY KILL (**29**).

Hammer into the floating rib — TO KILL (**30**).

Hammer fist to heart — TO KILL (**31**).

Hammer fist down hard on top foreskull (bregma) — TO KILL (**32**).

Hammer fist, either with hammer edge or top of fist using a pendulum swing (**33**) to the groin — TO KILL.

Hammer fist backhand into temple — TO KILL (**34**).

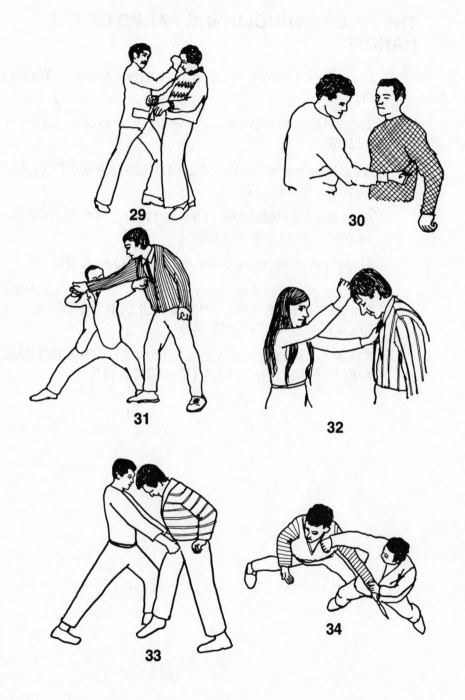

29

30

31

32

33

34

THE FINGERS (INCLUDING PALMS OF THE HANDS):

One handed choke, to crush the Adam's Apple — TO KILL (**35**).

Two handed thumb choke, pressing into esophagus — TO KILL (**36**).

Smash palms to ears — TO PUT OUT-OF-ACTION AND POSSIBLY KILL (**37**).

As is true for most blows, they can be applied from the rear as well as from the front (**38**).

Finger jab to the base of the throat — TO KILL (**39**).

A deep pinch to the trap muscle — TO TEMPORARILY PARALYZE THE ARM AND SHOULDER, IN ORDER TO FACILITATE A RELEASE (**40**).

Finger grab to the testicles — TO FACILITATE A RELEASE AND POSSIBLY PUT OUT-OF-ACTION (**41**).

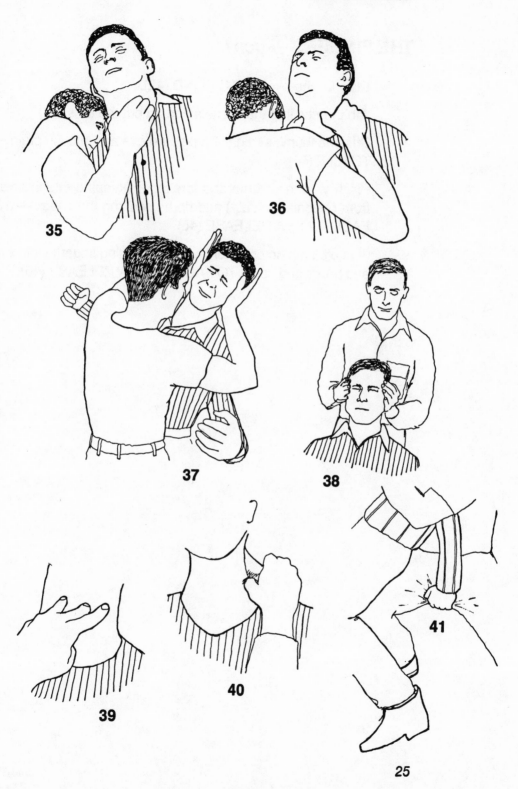

THE FINGERS — *con't.:*

Claw for the eyes — TO BLIND (**42**).

Jab thumbs into the sockets and rip out the orbs (**43**).

Drill one thumb straight through the eye and into the brain — TO KILL (**44**).

Pinch with the thumb and forefinger (keeping thumb away from opponent's teeth) and rip back along the cheek — TO FACILITATE A RELEASE (**45**).

Jam a thumb up opponent's nostril, digging finger(s) into eye and press and rip — TO FACILITATE A RELEASE (**46**).

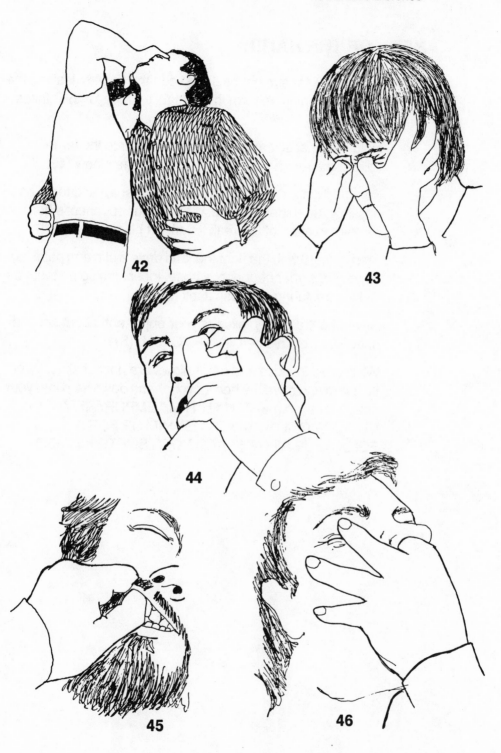

42

43

44

45

46

27

HEEL OF THE HAND:

Bend the wrist straight back and curl the fingers, leaving the base of the palm to form the contact surface for the strikes (**47**).

Hold the wrist stiff and drive up or down into the target, following through until the arm locks at the elbow (**48**).

For in-fighting, drive hard with as much snap and force as possible, up under the chin, driving your opponent's head back in an attempt to break it right off his vertebrae (**49**).

Step forward with the right foot and drive a stiff arm palm jab directly into your opponent's nose, loosening some teeth as well as fracturing the nose itself (**50**).

Drive into the solar plexus of your opponent, about second button up from his belt line — TO KILL (**51**).

When held in close and other blows are not possible, invert the palm and drive the heel of your hand down hard into your opponent's groin — TO PUT HIM TEMPORARILY OUT-OF-ACTION AND TO SET HIM UP FOR A FOLLOW-UP ATTACK, AND POSSIBLY TO KILL (**52**).

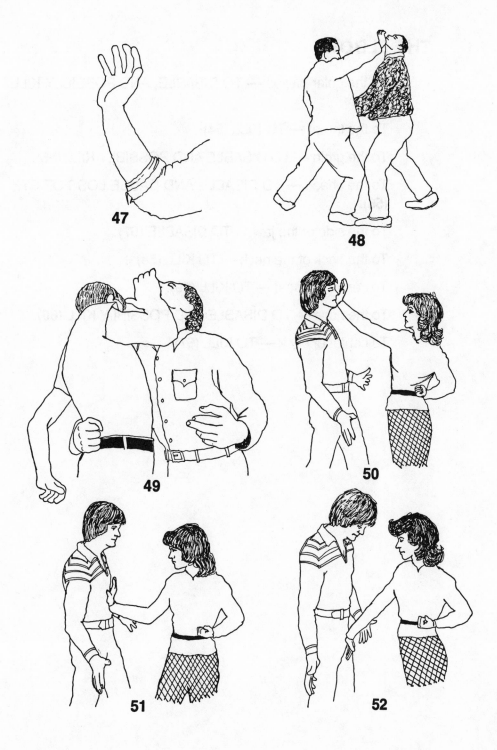

47

48

49

50

51

52

THE ELBOW:

To the solar plexus — TO DISABLE, AND POSSIBLY KILL **(53)**.

To the throat — TO KILL **(54)**.

To the groin — TO DISABLE AND POSSIBLY KILL **(55)**.

To the cheek — TO DISABLE AND CAUSE LOSS OF EYE **(56)**.

To the side of the jaw — TO DISABLE **(57)**.

To the back of the neck — TO KILL **(58)**.

To center of chest — TO KILL **(59)**.

To the nose — TO DISABLE AND POSSIBLY KILL **(60)**.

To center of back — TO KILL **(61)**.

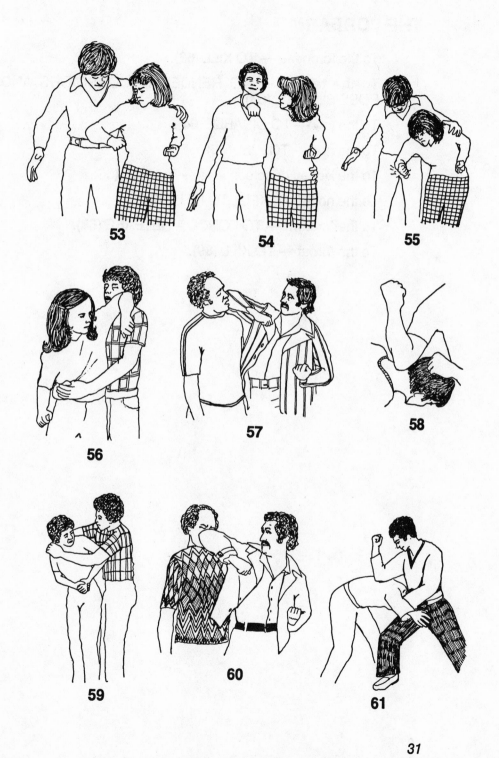

THE FOREARM:

To the forehead — TO KILL (**62**).

To the temple — TO RENDER UNCONSCIOUS AND POSSIBLY KILL (**63**).

To the jaw — TO DISABLE (**64**).

To the ribs — TO KILL (**65**).

To the kidney or spleen area — TO KILL (**66**).

To the nose — LIKELY TO KILL (**67**).

To the forearm — TO FORCE A RELEASE (**68**).

To the throat — TO KILL (**69**).

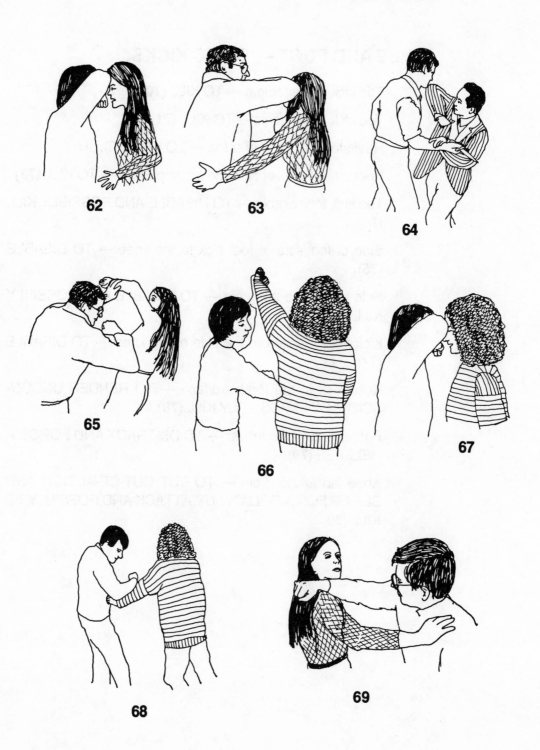

62

63

64

65

66

67

68

69

KNEE AND FOOT — BASIC KICKS:

Toe kick to the temple — TO KILL (**70**).

Toe kick to the heart — TO KILL (**71**).

Heel stomp to base of spine — TO KILL (**72**).

Heel crush to lower rib cage (solar plexus) — TO KILL (**73**).

Toe kick to the groin — TO DISABLE AND POSSIBLY KILL (**74**).

Side of foot/sole of foot kick to the knee — TO DISABLE (**75**).

Side toe kick to the groin — TO DISABLE AND POSSIBLY KILL (**76**).

Kick from the side to the side of the knee — TO DISABLE (**77**).

Knee kick to the forehead/face — TO RENDER UNCON-SCIOUS AND POSSIBLY KILL (**78**).

Foot stomp to the instep — TO DISTRACT AND FORCE A RELEASE (**79**).

Knee jab to the groin — TO PUT OUT-OF-ACTION AND SET UP FOR A FOLLOW-UP ATTACK AND POSSIBLY TO KILL (**80**).

70

71

72

73

74

75

76

77

78

79

80

KNEE AND FOOT — SPECIAL KICKS:

Toe kick to the heart — TO KILL (**81**).

Flat of sole-heel thrust to the solar plexus — TO RENDER A RELEASE AND POSSIBLY KILL (**82**).

Knee jab to the tail-bone — TO DISABLE TEMPORARILY AND SET UP FOR FOLLOW-UP ATTACK (**83**).

Flat of sole-heel back thrust to the knee — TO DISABLE (**84**).

Flat of sole-heel or edge of sole kick to the back of the leg — TO DISABLE (**85**).

Toe kick from the rear to the groin — TO DISABLE (**86**).

Reverse heel kick to the back — TO FORCE A RELEASE (**87**).

81

82

83

84

85

86

87

KNEE AND FOOT — SPECIAL KICKS — *con't.:*

Knee jab to the floating rib area — TO KILL (**88**).

Knee kick to the chest — TO PUT TEMPORARILY OUT-OF-ACTION AND SET UP FOR A FOLLOW-UP ATTACK (**89**).

Edge of sole scrape down shin — TO FORCE A RELEASE (**90**).

Kick to solar plexus from the ground — TO DISTRACT ENOUGH TO PERMIT FOLLOW-UP ATTACK (**91**).

Combination foot throw from the ground — TO DISABLE (**92**).

Sole of foot thrust from the ground — TO FORCE A RE-LEASE AND POSSIBLY PUT OUT OF ACTION (**93**).

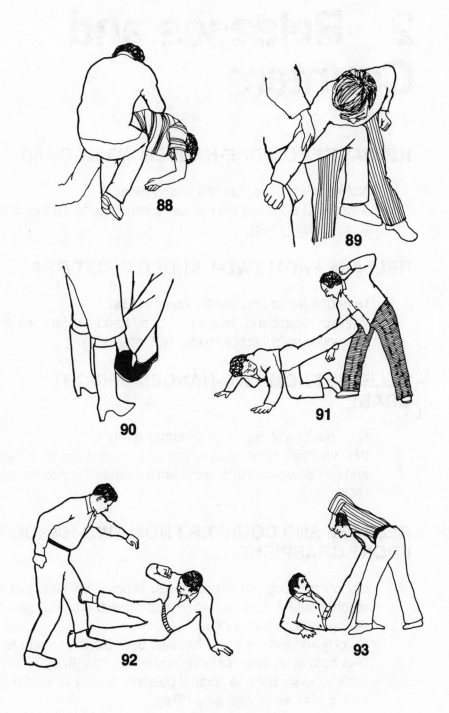

88

89

90

91

92

93

2 Releases and Counters

RELEASE FROM ONE-HANDED WRIST GRAB:

Note position of opponent's thumb (**94a**).
Twist wrist suddenly and violently into opponent's thumb to force release (**94b**).

RELEASE FROM TWO-HANDED WRIST GRAB:

Note position of opponent's thumbs (**95a**).
With your free hand grasp imprisoned hand and jerk upward into opponent's thumbs to force release (**95b**).

RELEASE FROM TWO-HANDED UPRIGHT GRAB:

Note position of opponent's thumbs (**96a**).
With your free hand, reach under and grasp imprisoned hand and jerk downward into opponent's thumbs to force release (**96b**).

RELEASE AND COUNTER FROM TWO-HANDED FRONT GRASP/CHOKE:

Opponent grasps throat or lapels, keeping his head out of reach of attack and holding you somewhat off balance hindering low kick attack (**97a**).
Quickly and with as much force as possible, swing one arm over both of his while pivoting and break hold (**97b**).
Pivot violently back to original position, driving an elbow attack to the head/throat area (**97c**).

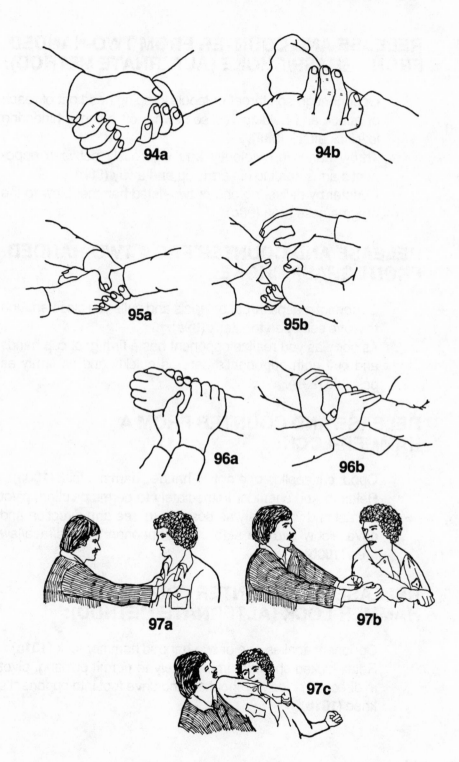

94a

94b

95a

95b

96a

96b

97a

97b

97c

RELEASE AND COUNTER FROM TWO-HANDED FRONT GRASP/CHOKE (ALTERNATE METHOD):

Opponent grasps throat or lapels keeping head out of reach of attack and holding you somewhat off balance hindering low kick attack (**98a**).

Throw hands up violently and vigorously between opponent's arms, forcing his arms up and away (**98b**).

Counter by delivering one or two-fisted hammer blow to the bregma/nose area (**98c**).

RELEASE AND COUNTER FROM TWO-HANDED FRONT GRASP/CHOKE:

Opponent grasps throat or lapels and pulls you close enough to leave self open to attack (**99a**).

As soon as you realize opponent has a firm grip, cup hands and cuff both opponent's ears as quickly and as firmly as possible (**99b**).

RELEASE AND COUNTER FROM A HAMMER-LOCK:

Opponent applies one or two-handed hammer lock (**100a**).

Relax locked shoulder immediately to permit pivoting, pivot as fast and vigorously as possible in free arm direction and drive elbow into the side of the opponent's head/face/jaw area (**100b**).

RELEASE AND COUNTER FROM HAMMER-LOCK (ALTERNATE METHOD):

Opponent applies one or two-handed hammer-lock (**101a**).

Relax locked shoulder immediately to permit pivoting, pivot in direction of locked shoulder and drive foot into opponent's knee (**101b**).

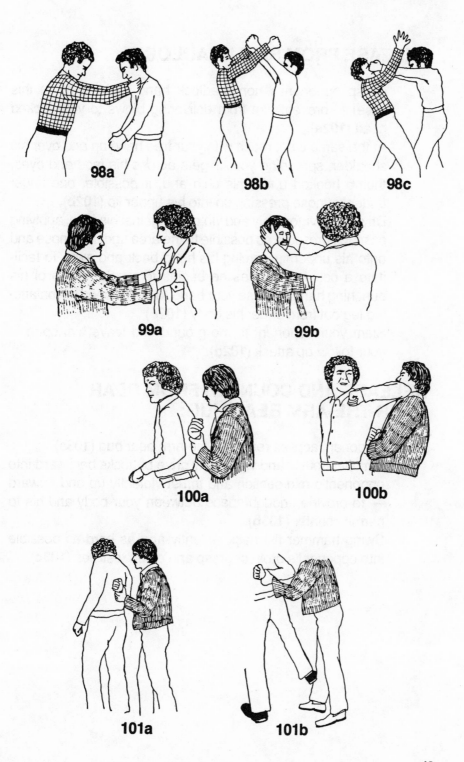

98a

98b

98c

99a

99b

100a

100b

101a

101b

RELEASE FROM SIDE HEADLOCK:

Grasp opponent's non-headlock hand (right hand in this case) to prevent him from delivering blows to your locked head **(102a)**.

At the same time, reach with your free hand up and over his shoulder, spreading your fingers across his face and eyes, thumb hooked under his chin and, if possible, one finger under his nose pressing up into his upper lip **(102b)**.

Drive back vigorously and violently against his face, applying as much pressure as possible to the area under his nose and onto his upper lip, forcing his head back and away to facilitate a counter. Just as he begins to topple, let go of his punching hand and use your hand to help sweep his balancing leg out from under his body **(102c)**.

Slam your opponent to the ground and leave him open to your follow-up attack **(102d)**.

RELEASE AND COUNTER FROM REAR OVER-THE-ARM BEAR HUG:

Opponent applies rear over-the-arm bear hug **(103a)**.

Simultaneously and vigorously drive buttocks backward into opponent's mid-section and thrust violently up and forward — to provide enough space between your body and his to permit counter **(103b)**.

Swing hammer fist back violently and as hard as possible into opponent's groin or grasp and crush testicles **(103c)**.

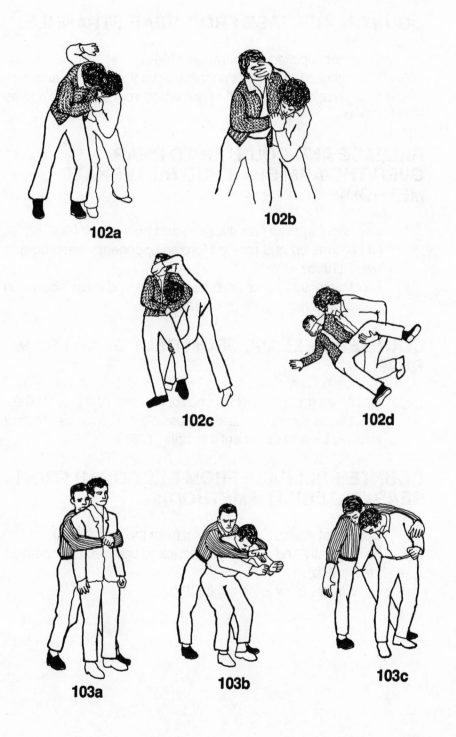

102a

102b

102c

102d

103a

103b

103c

COUNTER-RELEASE FROM REAR STRANGLE:

Opponent applies rear strangle (**104a**).
Violently and as hard as possible drive your arm up and over your shoulder with a stiff finger jab to your opponent's eyes (**104b**).

RELEASE AND COUNTER TO REAR OVER-THE-ARM BEAR HUG (ALTERNATE METHOD):

Opponent applies rear over-the-arm bear hug (**105a**).
Drive arms up and forward forcing opponent's arms up and away (**105b**).
Pivot violently and as hard as possible and drive elbow into opponent's floating rib area (**105c**).

COUNTER-RELEASE FROM BELT GRAB FROM REAR:

Opponent grabs belt, shirt, neck or hair from the rear (**106a**).
Pivot violently and as hard as possible and drive back hand/knuckle blow to opponent's temple (**106b**).

COUNTER-RELEASE FROM BELT GRAB FROM REAR (ALTERNATE METHOD):

Opponent grasps belt, hair, etc. from the rear (**107a**).
Pivot rapidly and deliver foot attack to opponent's knee/shin area (**107b**).
Or hammer blow to rib cage (**107c**).

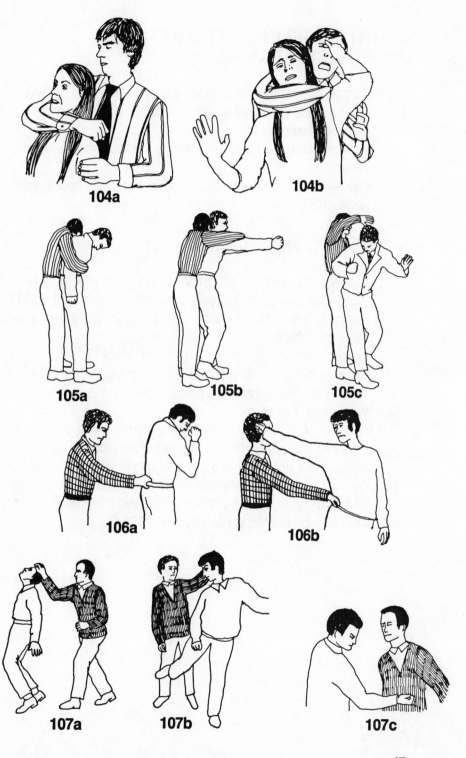

104a

104b

105a

105b

105c

106a

106b

107a

107b

107c

COUNTER-RELEASE FROM FRONT UNDER-ARM BEAR HUG:

Opponent applies front under-the-arm bear hug (**108a**).

Reach up and drive knuckles of either or both hands to opponent's temple (**108b**).

Or cup hands and cuff air violently into opponent's eardrums (**108c**).

Or drive knuckles of one or both hands into opponent's rib cage (**108d**).

A BASIC COUNTER-RELEASE:

Opponent applies a grasp from the front with one or both hands, or you catch his jab, or whatever else that suddenly lets you get both your hands on your opponent's wrist/forearm (**109a**).

Holding opponent's wrist firmly begin pivot (**109a**).

Draw opponent's arm forward and up under the pit of your own arm while continuing pivot, locking his arm into position with elbow (**109c**).

Let your legs move out and away from your body to prevent opponent's body from being fully twisted and turned free under your arm and slam him face down violently into the ground. Grasp opponent's hand in a wrist lock and apply pressure as necessary either to the wrist by bending or the shoulder by raising up on his arm. (**109d**).

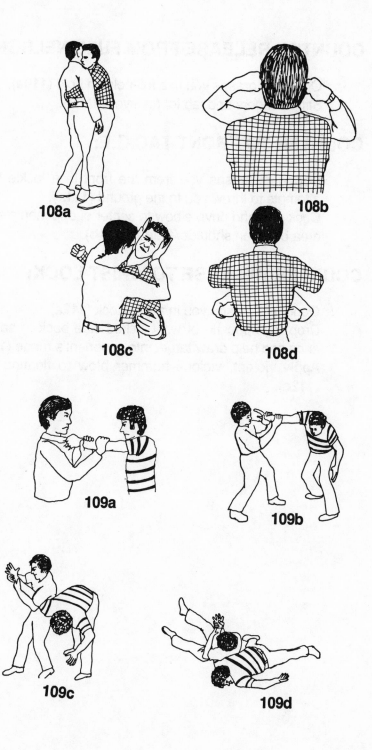

108a

108b

108c

108d

109a

109b

109c

109d

COUNTER-RELEASE FROM FULL-NELSON:

Opponent grasps you in a full-nels on hold (**110a**).
Stiffen fingers and jab for his eyes (**110b**).

COUNTER TO FRONT TACKLE:

Opponent grasps you from the front in a tackle hold and attempts to throw you to the ground (**111a**).
Cock arm and drive elbow to center of opponents spine into area between shoulder blades (**111b**).

COUNTER-RELEASE TO WRIST LOCK:

Opponent grasps you in a wrist lock (**112a**).
Drop leg opposite of wrist-locked side back to secure balance and help draw target into opponent's range (**112b**).
Apply violent, vicious hammer blow to floating rib area (**112c**).

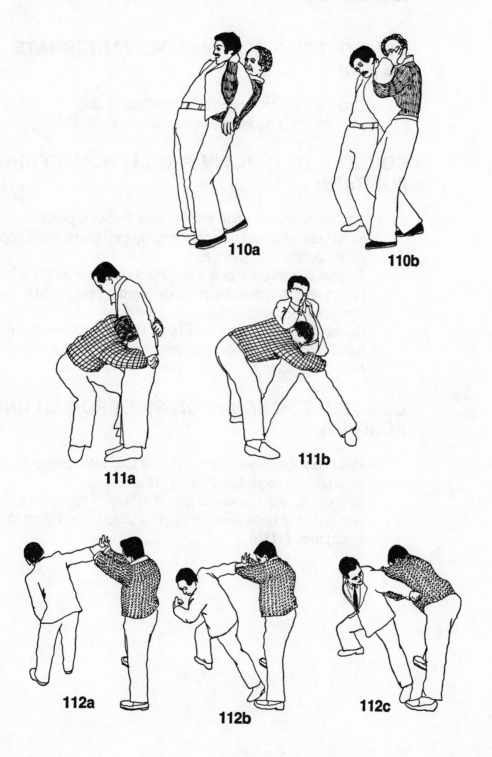

110a

110b

111a

111b

112a

112b

112c

COUNTER TO SIDE HEADLOCK (ALTERNATE METHOD):

Opponent grasps you in side headlock (**113a**).
Jab stiffened fingers into opponent's eyes (**113b**).

COUNTER TO THROWN PUNCH FROM SITTING POSITION:

You are seated in chair and attacker throws a punch at you. Keep your seat and do not attempt to get up and meet opponent's punch or to avoid it.

As punch is thrown, brace feet solidly on floor and block his punch with a crossed-arm-block, warding off the blow with the cross formed by your wrists (**114a**).

Deflect his punching arm with your left hand and drive a right hand/knuckle blow to opponent's temple area, across his nose, or chop to his throat (**114b**).

COUNTER TO GRAB-FROM-SIDE FROM SITTING POSITION:

Opponent grabs you from the side and attempts to lift you from chair in order to belt you (**115a**).

Smash out with backhand knuckle drive to opponent's temple, bridge of nose area, or swipe a vicious hard chop to his throat area (**115b**).

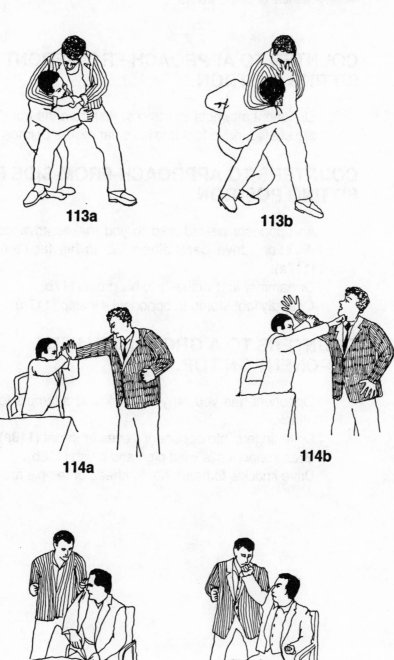

113a

113b

114a

114b

115a

115b

COUNTER TO APPROACH-FROM-FRONT FROM SITTING POSITION:

Opponent attempts to come at you from the front while you are seated, drive foot into his solar plexus or knee (**116**).

COUNTERS TO APPROACH-FROM-SIDE FROM SITTING POSITION:

An opponent seated next to you makes advances in your direction, drive back elbow jab to his face/throat areas (**117a**).
Or hammer first viciously to his groin (**117b**).
Or apply foot stomp to opponent's instep (**117c**).

COUNTERS TO A GROUND PIN WITH OPPONENT ON TOP:

Opponent has you on your back and attempts to force his attack.
Drive fingers into opponent's eyes or throat (**118a**).
Grasp opponent's wind pipe and crush (**118b**).
Drive knuckle to heart, rib, forehead or temple area (**118c**).

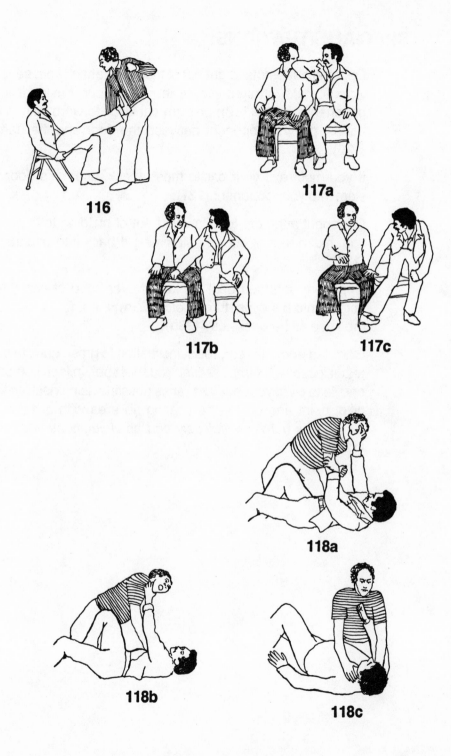

116

117a

117b   **117c**

118a

118b

118c

SPECIAL SITUATIONS:

Opponent attempts to get out of his car to attack you, send a vicious, hard, straight kick to the car's door, driving it into opponent's body (**119**); or slam car door forward with your hands, pinning opponent between the door and the frame (**120**).

If you must exit your car to meet attack, use car's door to slam into your opponent (**121**).

Opponent attempts to follow you out of building to confront you, make use of door by slamming it back into opponent. (**122**).

Opponent gets you bent backward over hood of car, drive fingers into his eyes, throat, etc (**123a**); then, follow-up with the knee as he backs off (**123b**).

Garroted from the rear, resist inclination to grasp garrote and tear it loose—*it's impossible.* Your best bet, in fact, you only one, is to pivot your body as far as possible using neck as the pivot point and go for the floating rib area with a hammer slam — *as hard, as viciously and as violently as you can.* (**124**).

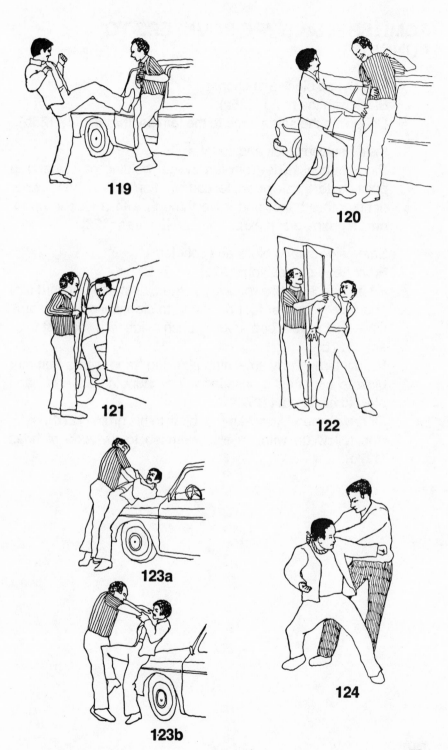

119

120

121

122

123a

123b

124

SOME SPECIAL TYPE COUNTERS TO PUNCHES:

The sweep block and chop:
Block with the hand (**125a**).
Chop with the same hand to the temple, throat, etc. (**125b**).

Inside sweep block and counter:
Block punch aside from the inside, holding other hand in position to block possible combination punch from opponent's other hand, and drive through with a kick to opponent's groin-solar plexus or knee-shin area (**126**).

Same side sweep block and counter:
From head-on position (**127a**).
When punch is thrown, pivot on the ball of your forward foot and drop your rear foot back and to side while at the same time striking your opponent's punch aside with your left forearm (**127b**).
Follow through by smashing blocking hand with a hammer blow to opponent's nose/face or a chopping edge of hand blow to his throat (**127c**).
Or drive a pendulum hammer blow to his groin (**127d**).
And follow up with an elbow smash to the side of head (**127e**).

125a **125b**

126

127a **127b** **127c**

127d **127e**

3 Natural Weapons Attack in Action

The following defenses are referred to as attacks. Once you are committed to your defense, you must commit yourself to aggressive action — driving, driving, driving — until your opponent is out of action.

1. Form a detailed list of those type of attacks or series of blows and kicks which are best suited to your temperament and abilities.
2. Keep your hands and feet moving constantly at your opponent's vital targets.
3. Go for the throat, eyes, solar plexus and groin as primary targets.
4. Low kicks are generally the best method of defensive attack — especially when your opponent is armed.
5. During the day, whenever the opportunity permits, rehearse your attacks in your mind's eye and practice them with an imaginary foe.

THE ATTACK #1:

Choose the attack *instantly* as your opponent begins to move in or as soon as he commits himself.
Drop into the fighting stance (**128a**).
Go for the throat (**128b**).
Follow up with a full elbow smash to the jaw (**128c**).
Follow through with the blow as with all blows (**128d**).
Then come back with an elbow smash up under the jaw and drive a fist into your opponent's solar plexus or groin to end it (**128e**).

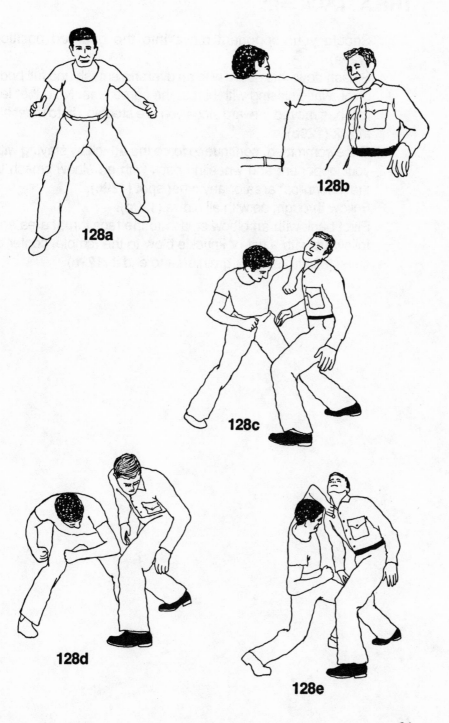

128a

128b

128c

128d

128e

THE ATTACK #2:

Should your opponent move into the guarded position (**129a**).

Smash down his guard with an overarm smash and full body pivot, while closing with him at the same time. Note that left foot has moved forward since you are stepping in to meet his attack (**129b**).

Once committed, continue to force the attack by staying with your opponent and wheeling back with an elbow smash to the face/throat area or any other spot (**129c**).

Follow through, as with all blows (**129d**).

Pivot back with an elbow smash to the face/throat area and follow-up with a fist or knuckle blow to the temple, center of chest, solar plexus or groin area to end it (**129e**).

129a

129b

129c

129d

129e

THE ATTACK #3 (FOOT ATTACK):

As opponent moves in, drop back onto rear leg, raising forward foot and dropping body back out of opponent's range of attack (**130a**).

Smash right leg out (forward leg) into opponent's knee, shin, groin, solar plexus or ribs (**130b**).

Follow-up with a wheeling edge-of-hand attack to the side of the neck or elbow to the temple to end it (**130c**).

130a

130b

130c

THE ATTACK #4:

If your opponent gets his hands on you, wheel with an over-the-arm release putting every bit of power into it (**131a**).
Slam down hard on his forearms and wrists, breaking the hold (**131b**).
Make a full body pivot and follow through (**131c**).
Then come back with an elbow smash, continuing the attack as shown in attack #1 and #2 to end it.

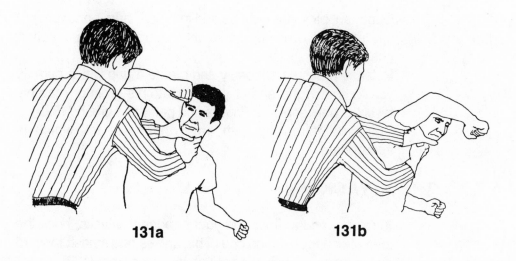

131a

131b

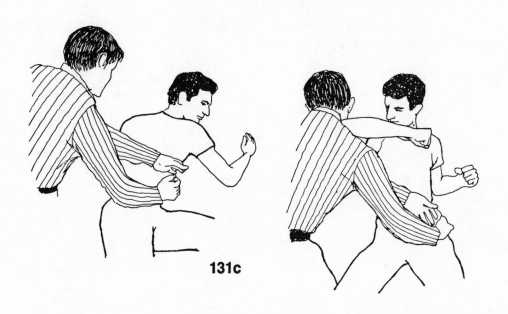

131c

THE ATTACK #5:

Opponent pins you from behind in a bear hug, bend forward sharply and drive buttocks into opponent's midsection (**132a**).

Release pressure suddenly and create a gap which permits you to smash the end of your fist into his groin or grab his testicles between your fingers and palm and crush (**132b**).

Spin and follow up with any forward attack which is appropriate.

THE ATTACK #6:

If you are on the floor and your opponent attacks, hook the toes of one foot behind one of his ankles and smash forward on his knee cap with the sole of your other foot (**133a**).

Holding the ankle foot firm, drive hard with the knee foot to dislocate your opponent's knee and to send him over backward onto the floor (**133b**).

Regain your feet immediately, and move-in and follow-up from a standing position.

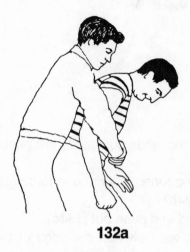

132a

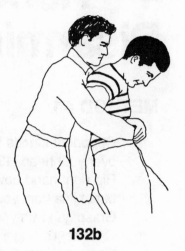

132b

133a

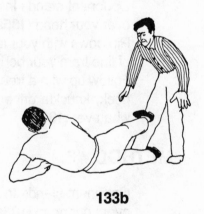

133b

4 Hand Gun Disarming

METHOD #1:

Opponent stands in front of you and your hands are raised over your head (**134a**).

Rip right hand down, grasp opponent's wrist and force gun out of line from your body (**134b**).

Grasp gun with your free hand and push out (**134c**).

Opponent's finger will be locked between the edge of the trigger and the trigger guard, putting him at your mercy and opening him up for a low level kick or knee attack (**134d**).

METHOD #2:

Opponent stands in front of you and your hands are raised over your head (**135a**).

Rip down with your left hand, grasping gun and forcing it out of line from your body (**135b**).

Follow up with a free hand edge-of-palm chop to opponent's neck, knuckle drive to his temple, toe kick to the groin or whatever (**135c**).

METHOD #3:

Opponent stands in front of you and your hands are raised over your head (**136a**).

Rip left hand down and force gun into opponent and out of line from your body, closing fingers around opponent's wrist (**136b**).

Drive free hand's fingers to opponent's throat or eyes, lay an edge of hand chop to the side of his neck, drive a knuckle into his chest, etc. (**136c**).

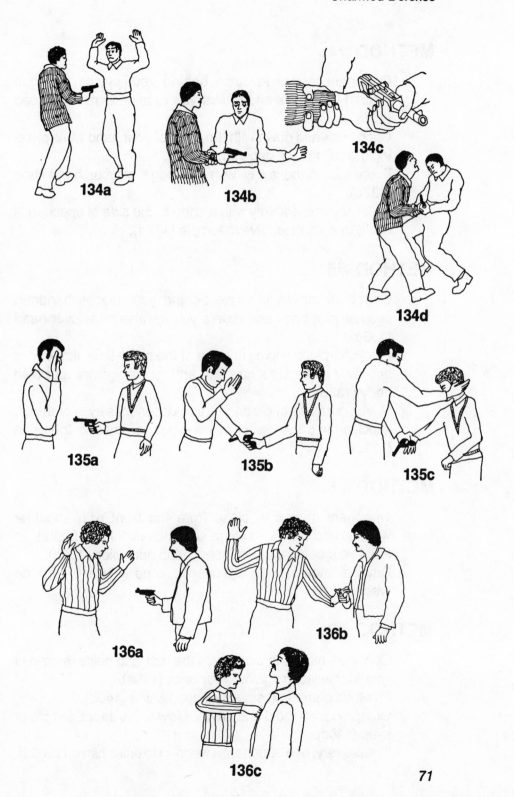

134a

134b

134c

134d

135a

135b

135c

136a

136b

136c

METHOD #4:

Opponent moves in close behind you, places handgun against your back and orders you to raise arms over head (**137a**).

Chop back and down with the edge of your hand while pivoting around to face opponent (**137b**).

Force gun hand away with the edge of your hand-chop (**137c**).

Follow-up immediately with a chop to the side of opponent's neck, or a knuckle drive to temple (**137d**).

METHOD #5:

Opponent moves in close behind you, places handgun against your back and orders you to raise arms over head (**138a**).

Pivot sharply, stepping in close at the same time; throw your arm over opponent's gun arm and lock it against your own body (**138b**).

Drive your free hand's fingers into opponent's eyes or throat, knuckles into the center of his chest, or knee to the groin (**138c**).

METHOD #6:

Opponent moves in close from the front with shoulder weapon and orders you to raise hands over head (**139a**).

Pivot your body at the waist and slap gun aside (**139b**).

Drive a knee kick to opponent's knee — *Keep Grip on Weapon* (**139c**).

METHOD #7:

Opponent moves in close from the rear and holds muzzle of shoulder weapon against your back (**140a**).

Pivot, drop arm and smack weapon aside (**140b**).

Grasp weapon, hold and drive a blow to his throat, temple or eyes (**140c**).

If necessary, use opponent's weapon to finish him off (**140d**).

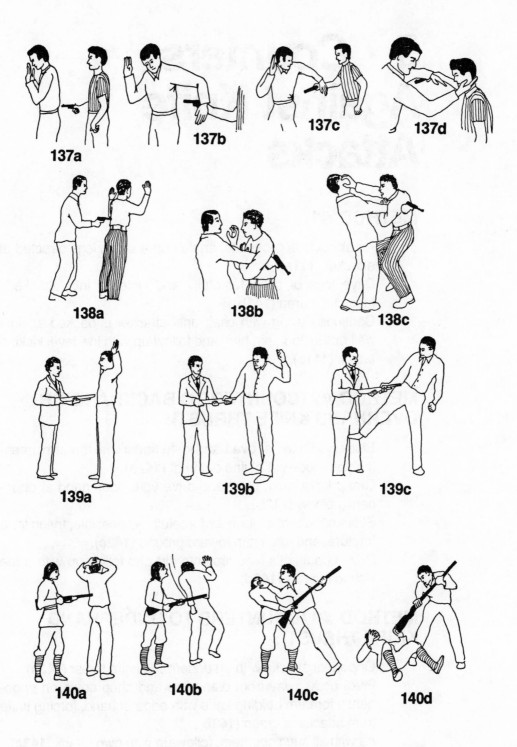

137a

137b

137c

137d

138a

138b

138c

139a

139b

139c

140a

140b

140c

140d

5 Counters Against Knife Attacks

METHOD #1:

As attacker approaches, snatch up a chair, legs directed at attacker (**141a**).

Drive legs of chair forcefully and violently into attacker's face/chest area (**141b**).

Continue driving with chair until attacker is backed against wall or the floor; pin him, and follow-up with low level kicking attack (**141c**).

METHOD #2 (COUNTER TO BACKHAND OR OVERHAND KNIFE THRUST):

Block backhand or overhand knife thrust with forearm, keeping your body out of line of thrust (**142a**).

Grasp knife wrist, pivot and drive your open hand at opponent's elbow (**142b**).

Strike opponent's elbow as forcefully as possible, trying for a fracture, and force him toward ground (**142c**).

Drive opponent's face first into dirt and follow-up with a toe kick to the ribs (**142d**).

METHOD #3 (COUNTERS TO UNDERHAND KNIFE THRUST):

Opponent attacks with an underhand knife thrust (**143a**).

Pivot body away from blade line and chop down on opponent's forearm holding knife with edge of hand, forcing knife from attacker's grasp (**143b**).

As with all such counters, follow-up with own attack (**143c**).

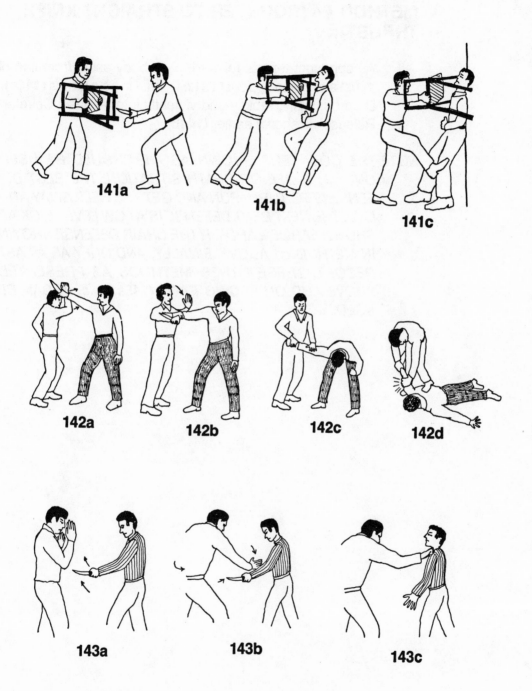

141a

141b

141c

142a

142b

142c

142d

143a

143b

143c

METHOD #4 (COUNTER TO STRAIGHT KNIFE THRUST):

As opponent thrusts forward, pivot body aside from line of thrust and grasp opponent's knife wrist in both hands (**144a**). Drop smoothly, rapidly and violently into 'A Basic Counter-Release' as shown earlier (**144b**).

NOTE: *THE COUNTERS SHOWN ABOVE SHOULD BE USED ONLY IN A LIFE OR DEATH SITUATION. THE BEST DEFENSE IS TO TURN, RUN AND GET THE HELL AWAY AND LIVE. THE NEXT BEST DEFENSE IS A LOW LEVEL KICK AS SHOWN EARLIER AND/OR THE CHAIR DEFENSE SHOWN IN METHOD #1 ABOVE. FINALLY, AND ONLY AS A LAST RESORT, THESE OTHER METHODS AS PRESENTED ABOVE AND ON FACING PAGE (145a, b, c, d) CAN BE USED.*

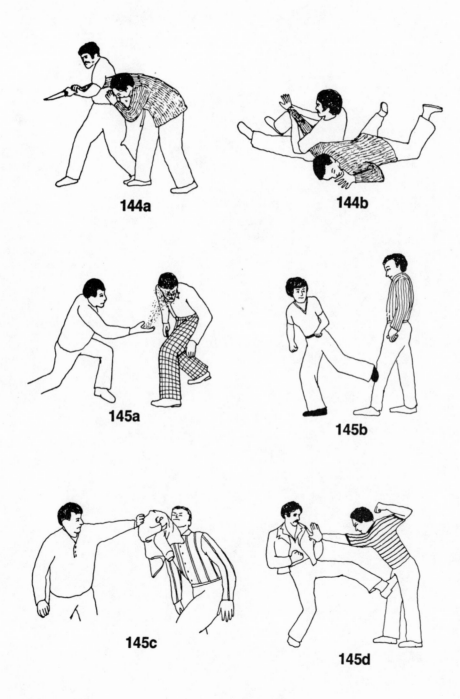

144a

144b

145a

145b

145c

145d

II Armed Defense

6 Weapons

POINTS TO REMEMBER CONCERNING WEAPONS:

Your decision to use a lethal or non-lethal weapon must be based upon individual need.

You must understand how to use it and how to care for it — *safely*.

Before using, you must decide that you can kill when necessary or else forget it.

Consider the legal aspects of ownership in your locale, etc., and weigh these against the need, BEFORE FINALIZING YOUR DECISION.

LETHAL WEAPONS:

1. Shotgun:
   Excellent for close self defense.
   Generally legal in all U.S. States and Territories as well as in most other areas overseas, as a sporting weapon.
   Generally safe around dwellings.
   Best for self defense is a 5-shot automatic or pump.
2. Rifle:
   Not as effective as shotgun in close quarters, but more effective at longer ranges.
   Excellent against attacks from outside residence.
   Has greater penetrating power than shotgun. If forced to use inside residence, a rifle slug will generally penetrate walls.
3. Handguns (Revolvers, Pistols, etc.):
   Excellent close-in weapon for self defense, and personal protection at home or in the streets.
   Must be located where user has efficient rapid access to it.
   Purchase only high quality and reputable make.
   Insure weapon is double action.
   Best for self defense is .38 caliber or larger, i.e., .44, .45, or 9MM.
   Generally unsafe around children or others who have no knowledge of such weapons and therefore must be secured from them in a location inaccessible to them.

NON-LETHAL WEAPONS:

1. Taser or Electric Gun (**146a, b**):
   Immobilizes immediately.
   Effective range is 6-8 feet.
   Aims like a flashlight.
   Fires two small darts which imbed in the target's clothing, permitting an electric current (50,000 volts) to pass instantaneously from gun to target.
   Does not affect pacemakers, the heart, nor permit electrocution of user or target, even if standing in water — *but injury from fall once rendered immobile or from after-effects is not precluded* (always refer to manufacturing details for specific guarantees, warnings, etc.).
   CHECK LOCAL LAWS BEFORE USE.

2. Chemical Sprays:
   Blind attacker temporarily. *Not recommended for use against armed assailant(s), unless used in conjunction with a lethal weapon,* but better than nothing in a life-or-death situation.
   CS (orthochlorobenzalmalononitrite) is *best* and is sold under the trade name of *Shield* (**147**).
   Effective against multiple attackers.
   Functions under all weather conditions.
   Range 5-8 feet.
   Incapacitates for 5-10 minutes.
   Unobtrusive.
   Can be fired from holster.
   Totally non-lethal.
   CHECK LOCAL LAWS BEFORE USE.

3. Bright Light (**148**):
   Effective only in dark.
   Radiates 5 million lumens candle power.
   Blinds attacker(s) for approximately 24 hours.
   Generally best to use in conjunction with a back-up weapon.

4. Electic Prod (**149**):
   Provides up to 6,000 volts.
   Use in conjunction with a back-up weapon.
   CHECK LOCAL LAWS BEFORE USE.

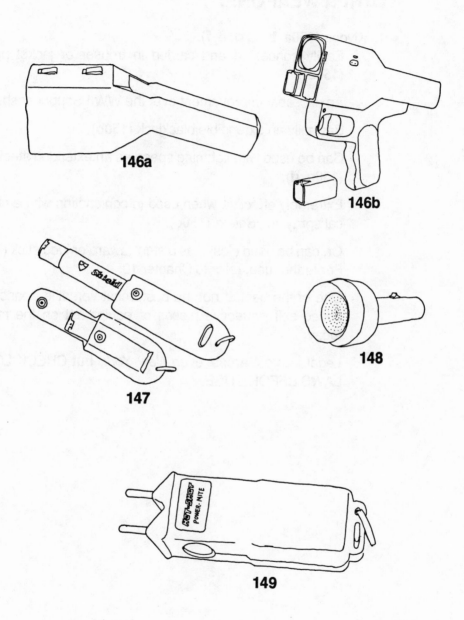

146a

146b

147

148

149

OTHER WEAPONS:

1. Kiyoga (**150a, b, c, d, e, f**):

Easily concealed and carried in trouser or jacket pocket (**150a**).

An excellent improvement over the WWII Sapper cosh.

Basically an extendible blackjack (**150b**).

Can be used with lightning speed as an extended steel whip (**150c, d**).

Extremely effective when used in conjunction with a chemical spray, ie., *Shield* (**150e**).

Or, can be used closed as a steel jawara or judo stick (**150f**). For further use, refer to Chapter 10.

One of the best, if not the best, most versatile, reasonably priced self protective pieces of equipment on the market today.

Legal in most areas, *even New York,* but CHECK LOCAL LAWS BEFORE USE.

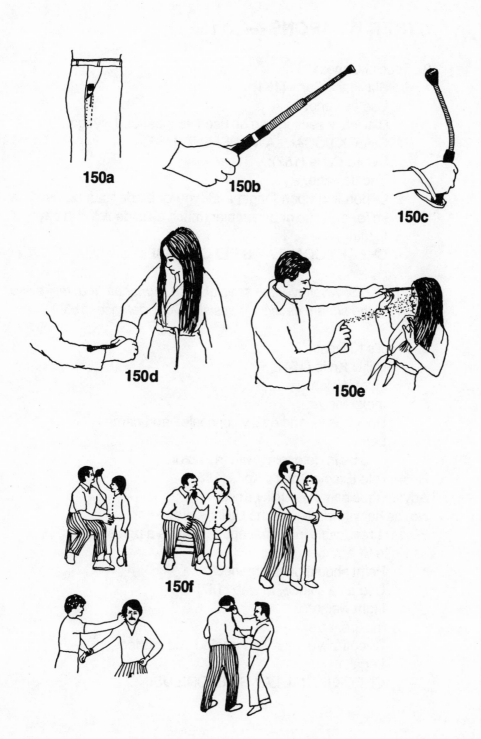

150a

150b

150c

150d

150e

150f

OTHER WEAPONS — *con't.:*

2. Special Canes:
> Blackjack Cane (**151**):
> Use as cane.
> Blackjack section can be used as extended kiyoga.
> CHECK LOCAL LAWS BEFORE USE.
> Sword Cane (**152**):
> Use as cane.
> Depending upon length and type of blade, can be used as knife, a stiletto or as a rapier (much as is depicted in bayonet fighting).
> CHECK LOCAL LAWS BEFORE USE.

> *NOTE: Whenever the special cane is unsheathed, make use of the sheath section to assist in your defense (**153**).*

3. Artist's Knives:
> Utility Knife (**154**):
> Light Weight.
> Inexpensive.
> Unobtrusive and easily concealed and carried.
> Legal.
> Use as in defending with the razor.

Retractible Exacto Artist's Knife (**155**):
Advantages same as Utility Knife.
Not as heavily bladed as the Utility Knife.
Blade is retractible into what appears to be a pen shell.

4. Knife Sharpener (**156**):
> Point should be sharpened
> Use as a stiletto, to stab (**157**).
> Light weight.
> Inexpensive.
> Unobtrusive, easily concealed and carried.
> Legal.
> CHECK LOCAL LAWS BEFORE USING.

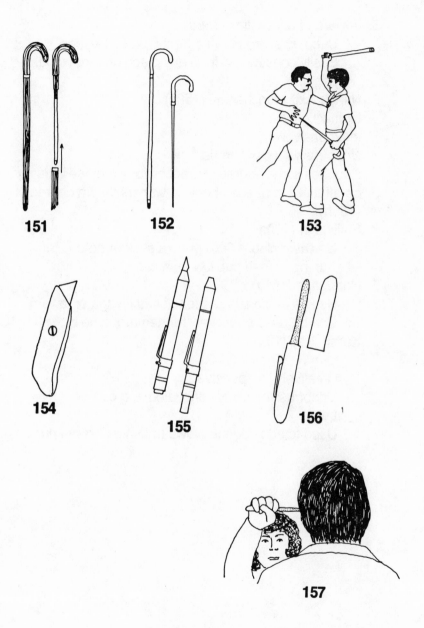

151

152

153

154

155

156

157

OTHER WEAPONS — *con't.:*

5. Jawara or Judo Stick (**158**):
    Used as demonstrated for the closed kiyoga.
    Easily constructed from any piece of hard wood.
    Legal.
6. Nunchacku (nunchacks) (**159a**):
    Lightweight.
    Inexpensive.
    Unobtrusive, easily carried.
    Requires some degree of practice for expertise in usage, but can be effective in hands of novice with minimum degree of practice (**159b**).
7. Shillelagh (**160a**):
    Use as a club (**160b**) or as a stick or baton.
    Can be carried publicly as a cane.
8. Handgrips (**161a**):
    Use as demonstrated for closed kiyoga or jawara.
    Can be used effectively for hammer type blows (**161b**).
9. Karate Key (**162**):
    Light.
    Relatively inexpensive.
    Unobtrusive, easily concealed and carried.
    Legal.
    Used to add edge to blows (much as brass knuckles).

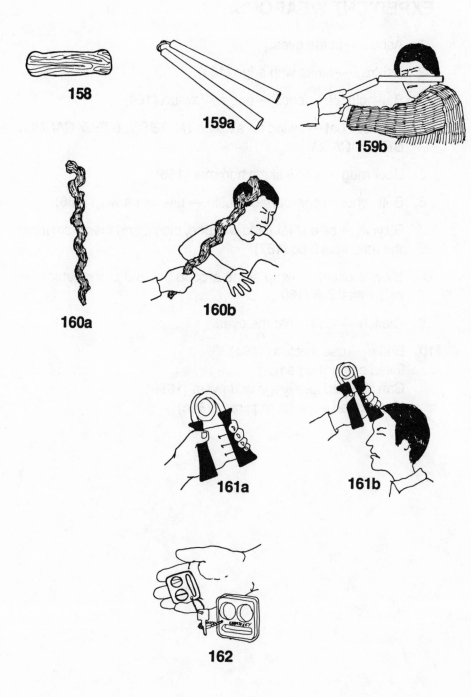

158

159a

159b

160a

160b

161a

161b

162

EXPEDIENT WEAPONS:

1. Ashes — in the eyes.

2. Ashtray — strike with edge (**163**).

3. Ball-point pen/pencil — use as Jawara (**164**).

4. Baseball bat — swing for a homer; *IT ABSOLUTELY CANNOT BE BLOCKED.*

5. Beer mug — use it like a hammer (**165**).

6. Belt w/heavy sharpened buckle — use like a whip (**166**).

7. Bicycle — as a shield and weapon; block, and then slam it into the attackers face (**167**).

8. Bicycle chain — wrap some around fist and swing remainder as a lethal flail (**168**).

9. Bleach — toss it into the eyes.

10. Bottle — use as club (**169a**).
    Filled better than empty.
    Can be used as Kiyoga or Jawara (**169b**).
    Use jagged edge as required (**169c**).

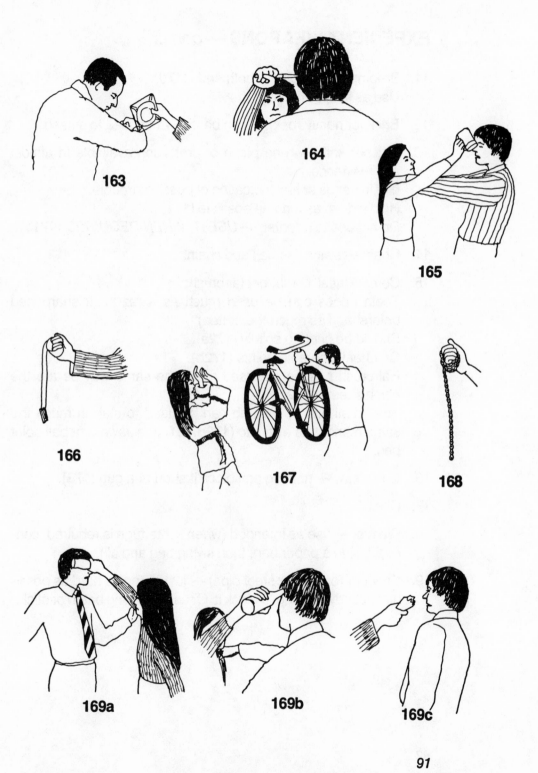

163

164

165

166

167

168

169a

169b

169c

EXPEDIENT WEAPONS — *con't.:*

11. Broom — make use of both ends (**170**).
    Use as in stick fighting.

12. Brick (or heavy rock) — can be thrown or used to smash.

13. Butcher knife — one piece of protection available in almost any residence:
    Get in hands at first indication of possible trouble.
    Hold hidden as long as possible (**171a**).
    Do not use to threaten — *USE IT, WHEN REQUIRED* (**171b**).

14. Chain — swing like ball and chain.

15. Comb, Rattail comb, or Hairbrush:
    Teeth edges can be used much as a razor. (If sharpened beforehand so much the better.)
    Should be gripped solidly (**172a**).
    Go after vulnerable points (**172b**).
    Hairbrush bristles are used much the same way as are the comb's teeth (**172c**).
    The rattail end of a comb can be used to stab in much the same manner as a stiletto (**172d, e, f**) or a Jawara or ball point pen.

16. Chain saw — nothing can block it short of a gun (**173**).

17. Chair.

18. Cleaver — use as intended (when subterfuge is required, conceal inside a paper bag, then swing bag and all).

19. Crowbar (or lead or steel pipe) — just swing as hard as possible; nobody is going to block it. Or use as a long baton or stick.

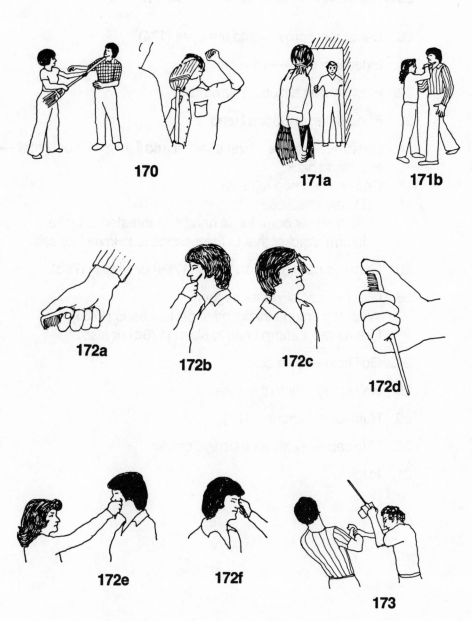

170

171a

171b

172a

172b

172c

172d

172e

172f

173

EXPEDIENT WEAPONS — *con't.:*

20.   Deodorant spray — into the eyes (**174**).

21.   Extension cord — as a garrote.

22.   Flashlight as a club, or Jawara.

23.   Fork, Knife, or Spoon Handle.

24.   Gasoline — douse it over attacker and light match or lighter — and stand back.
      Can be used non-lethally:
         Douse attacker.
         Hold lighter or match in hand and threaten to ignite.
         Inform attacker that to fire weapon is to immolate self.

25.   Garbage can lid — can throw (**175a**) or swing (**175b**).

26.   Glass — use sliver as dagger:
      Wrap rag around thick end to protect hand (**176a**).
      Use as razor sharp knife to slash (**176b**) or stab.

27.   Golf club — as a club.

28.   Hair spray — into the eyes.

29.   Hatchet or hammer (**177**).

30.   Hub cap — same as garbage can lid.

31.   Icepick.

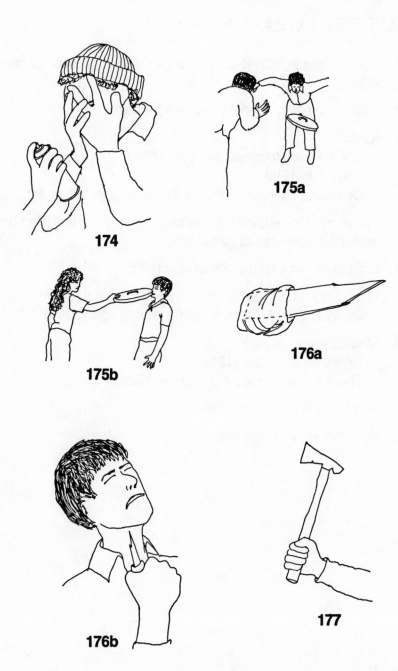

174

175a

175b

176a

176b

177

EXPEDIENT WEAPONS — *con't.:*

32. Iron — smash with it as you would with a brick or hammer (**178**).

33. Jack handle (lug wrench) — use as a club.

34. Keys:
    Can be used to attack the eyes (**179a**).
    The neck (**179b**).
    Or other vulnerable points of the body (see appendix).

35. Letter opener — use as a stiletto or other sharp stabbing type object, i.e., pen, rattail comb, etc.

36. Light bulb — crush glass into face (**180**).

37. Lubricant (spray type) and match — as flame thrower:
    Spray and light match or lighter next to spray (**181**).

38. Magazine:
    Rolled as a Jawara (**182a**).
    The edge flicked up into the eye (**182b**).

39. Paint — tossed into the eyes.

40. Pitchfork — as a bayonet.

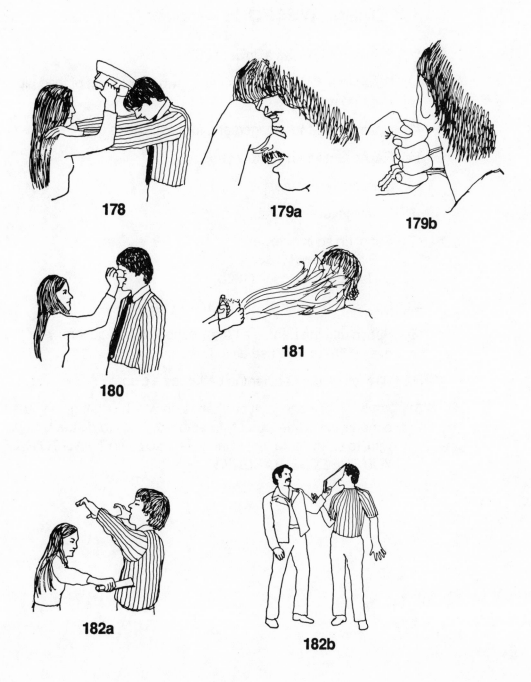

178

179a

179b

180

181

182a

182b

EXPEDIENT WEAPONS — *con't.:*

41. Pocket Knife — as a Jawara (**183**).

42. Poker from fireplace — use as crowbar or length of lead pipe, to swing with.

43. Rake — use the pronged end for best results (**184**).

44. Razor, Straight or Safety (**185**).

45. Scissors — to stab.

46. Screwdriver — to stab.

47. Soap: (in sock or towel)
    Place in towel (**186a**).
    Use as a blackjack (**186b**).

48. Spade — use same as a pitchfork (**187**).

49. Spoon use the handle as the weapon and go generally for the eyes (**188**) or else use as a Jawara.

50. Wrench — the heavier the better, as a club.

51. Anything you can lay your hands on which might give you an edge in the battle, to cut, to stab, to blind, to distract, to jab with, to strangle, to trip, whatever — *BUT ANYTHING TO GIVE YOU THE EDGE TO SURVIVE.*

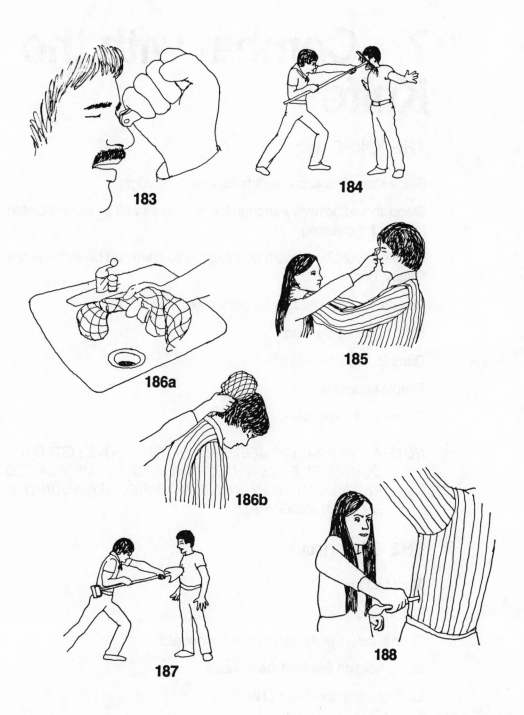

183

184

186a

185

186b

187

188

7   Combat with the Knife

THE KNIFE (189):

Blade should be capable of holding a keen edge.

Blade should be heavy enough for hacking as well as sharp-pointed enough for stabbing.

Handle should be smooth and straight so knife can be thrown from fighting grip.

Requires hand guard for for protection.

Must be well-balanced.

Durable.

Simple structure.

Relatively inexpensive.

NOTE: A KNIFE WHICH MEETS ALL OF THE ABOVE LISTED RE-QUIREMENTS IS THE STANDARD HEAVY BLADED KABAR BUTCHER KNIFE MODIFIED BY ADDING A BRASS HANDGUARD.

THE GRIP (190):

Must be firm.

Wrist locked.

Thumb down, protected by the handguard.

Blade held on line with the forearm.

Cutting edge down — *ALWAYS.*

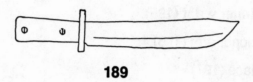

189

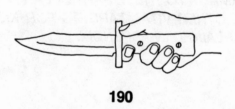

190

TARGETS:

Base of the throat **(191)**.

The stomach **(192)**.

The heart **(193)**.

The inner thigh **(194)**

The inner wrist (195).

The upper arm **(196)**.

The face **(197)**

The side of the neck **(198)**.

The temple **(199)**.

The small of the back **(200)**.

NOTE: DAMAGE TO THESE PARTICULAR LOCATIONS AS WELL AS OTHER VITAL TARGETS FOR KNIFE ASSAULT ARE EXPLAINED IN APPENDIX.

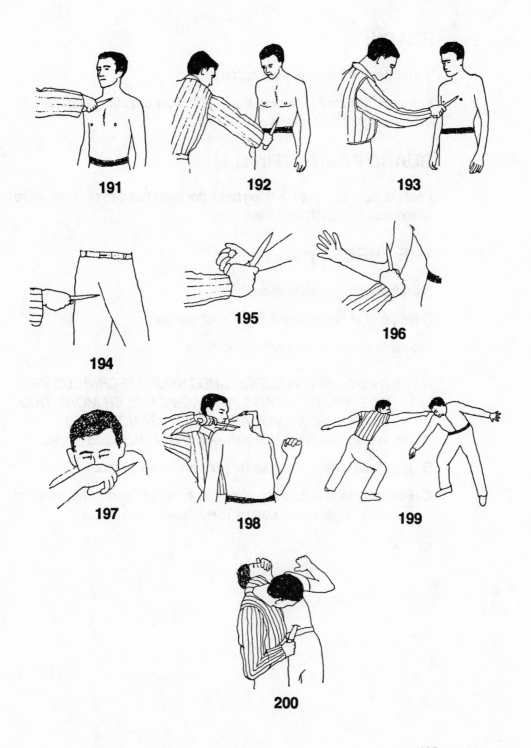

191 192 193

194 195 196

197 198 199

200

REACH:

Your effective range is your reach.

You should know it from both the left-foot forward stance (**201a**) and from the right-foot forward stance (**201b**).

GUARD POSITION (202a, b):

Feet comfortably apart, left leg back (for right-handed person), knife arm drawn back, left arm free.

THE THRUST (203a, b):

Start from the guard position.

Drive point of blade straight into your attacker.

Free arm snaps to the rear during drive.

*NOTE: THIS GUARD POSITION AND THRUST TECHNIQUE PRO-
VIDE AN ADVANTAGE IN REACH OF OVER MORE THAN
15-20 INCHES OVER ANY OTHER STANCE. PLUS:*

A. Insures shortest distance between end of blade and target.

B. Is difficult to block or counter from any other stance.

C. Presents side silhouette of self to enemy's blade (the smallest possible target which can be presented).

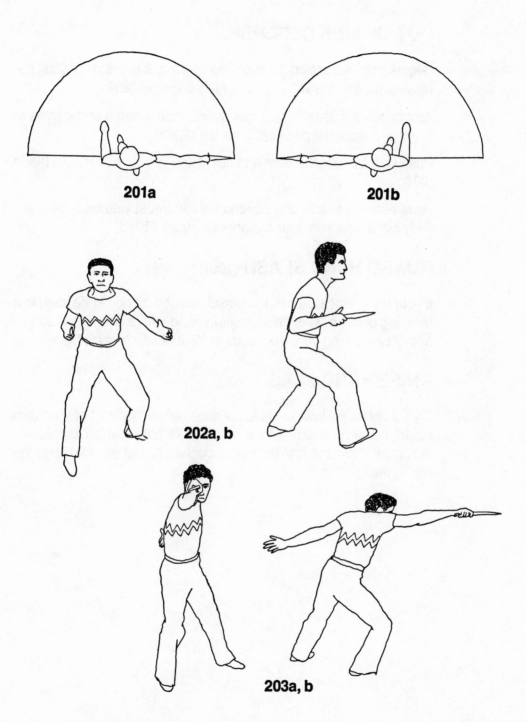

201a   **201b**

202a, b

203a, b

OUT OF LINE DEFENSE:

Begins from the guard position (concealing the nature of your defense until target is within your effective range) (**204a**).

As opponent rushes into range, thrust knife forward at the eyes of opponent, applying power to your leg (**204b**).

Push your body to the right and out of line of your opponent's blade (**204c**).

Plant rear leg solidly and continue blade thrust with body now entirely out of line with your opponent's attack (**204d**).

GUARD HAND SLASH (205):

If your opponent assumes the guard stance with non-knife hand in a blocking posture, slash his blocking hand with a downward sabre-hack, maintaining your own body still out of reach of his blade.

KNIFE HAND SLASH (206):

If your opponent lowers his knife hand below the level of your own blade, consider a sabre-hack to his knife hand, which should not only disarm him but distract him enough to permit you to deliver the final blow.

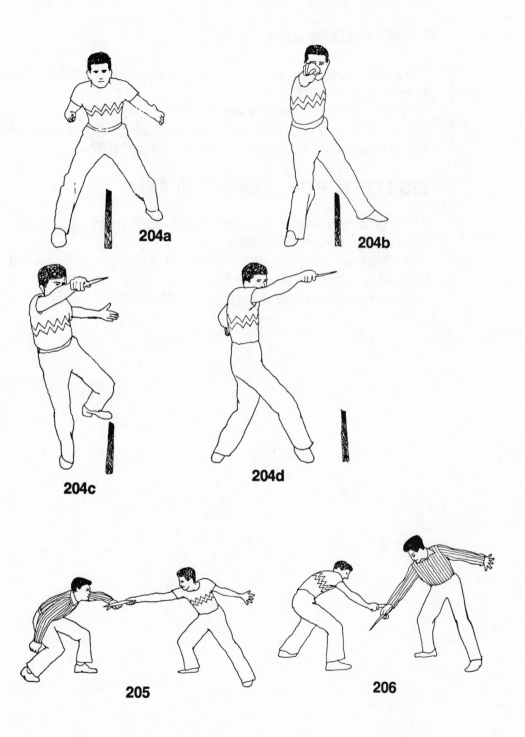

204a

204b

204c

204d

205

206

FEINT AND SLASH:

Feint with a low, short thrust triggering your opponent to flinch his knife hand back (**207a**).
Whip your blade up toward your opponent's eyes (**207b**).
And slash across his eyes and forehead, putting him out of action and setting him up for the finishing blow or thrust (**207c**).

SIDE OF THROAT/TEMPLE SLASH:

If your opponent attacks in such a manner as to permit you to get a hand on his knife arm wrist (**208**).
Brace his wrist with your arm and, instead of attempting an upward thrust to the stomach which he might block, slash across his neck/temple area which will end the attack — *PERMANENTLY.*

207a

207b

207c

208

COUNTER SLASH TO THE LONG THRUST:

Should your opponent attempt a long thrust (**209a**) or any type upward thrust, slash with a sabre-hack to disarm and set him up for a finishing blow or thrust (**209b**).

COUNTER TO THE OVERHAND ATTACK:

Should any opponent be so foolish to attempt an overhand attack as shown, drop low and thrust the blade into his chest/abdomen area (**210**).

NOTE:WHEN YOU PRACTICE THE KNIFE FIGHTING TECH-NIQUES DEPICTED IN THIS SECTION: REVIEW THE PHYSICAL IMPLICATIONS OF BLOWS IN THE APPENDIX.

209a

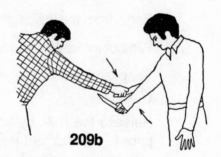

209b

210

Knife Throwing

NOTE:Once a knife is thrown, for all practical purposes it is gone. THEREFORE, IT IS USUALLY A BETTER CHOICE TO KEEP THE KNIFE AND FIGHT WITH IT THAN TO THROW IT AT YOUR OPPONENT.

GRIP:

Use the same basic grip as indicated for knife fighting (**211**). Any basic change in stance or grip might warn your opponent of your intent to throw before fighting.

BASIC THROW:

Begin from the knife fighting guard position (**212a**).

Without indicating your intent, whip arm back suddenly (**212b**).

Snap arm forward vigorously, with as much power as possible (**212c**).

Release the knife by letting handle slide smoothly from hand just prior to the moment that your arm arrives at a point exactly level with your shoulder (**212d**).

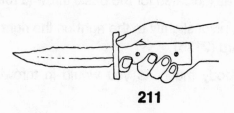

211

212a

212b

212c

212d

ALTERNATE OVERHAND METHOD:

Use the same basic grip as indicated for the basic throw (**213a**).

From the guard position, pivot slightly to the right on the right foot, cocking the left leg forward (**213b**).

Drive forward with the body much as you would in throwing a baseball (**213c**).

Release the knife by letting the handle slip smoothly from your grasp at the horizontal level and follow through just as you would when throwing a baseball (**213d**).

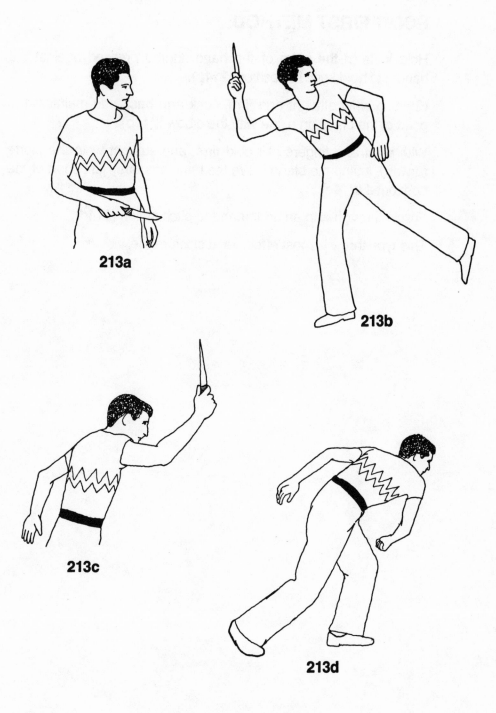

213a

213b

213c

213d

POINT FIRST METHOD:

Hold knife in the palm of the hand, thumb pressed against the handle to hold knife in position (**214a**).

Keeping wrist straight and firm, cock arm back and maintain the point of the blade on a line with the elbow (**214b**).

With wrist and fingers still held firm, and straight whip the blade forward, letting the blade leave the hand smoothly just short of the horizontal (**214c**).

Follow through with an underhanded-pitch action (**214d**).

This type throw is most effective at close range.

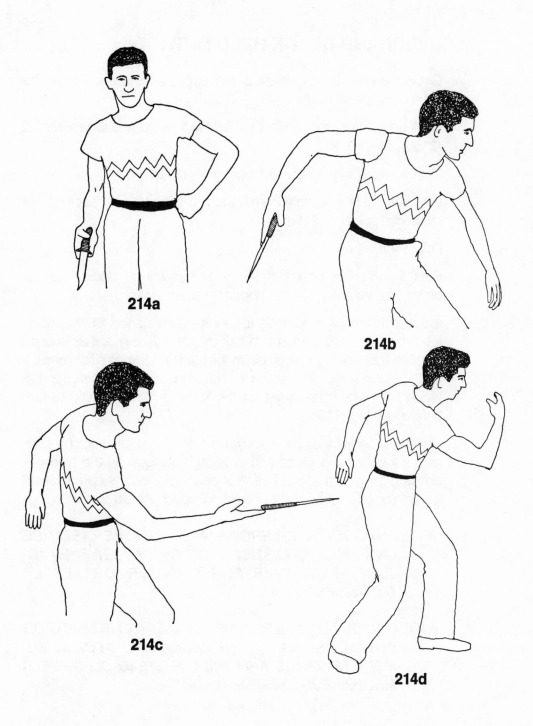

214a

214b

214c

214d

OVERHAND BLADE-HELD METHOD:

Grasp the knife by the blade, *sharp edge out and away from the palm of the hand* (**215a**).

Cock body back on the right foot, left leg forward and slightly raised (**215b**).

Drive forward with a baseball-type throw (**215c**).

Let blade slide smoothly from hand just prior to arm reaching the horizontal position (**215d**).

Follow through.

Put full power into each throw — *even if your knife does not strike blade first, you may still put opponent out-of-action.*

Practice this throw repeatedly to gauge your distance. Start by holding knife with fingers and thumb as close to hand-guard as is comfortable and adjust your grip down the blade until knife sticks consistently to your target. The average six foot male should allow approximately 5 yards from target for the knife to make exactly ½ turn before sticking (**215e**).

Once your basic distance is known, increase your distance by stepping backward two yards and lowering your grip on the blade — allowing for a turn and a half. For each additional step backward lower your grip slightly further down the blade (**215f**).

NOTE: *PRACTICE ALL THROWS AT ONLY ONE DISTANCE UNTIL YOU CONSISTENTLY HIT THE TARGET; THEN ADJUST YOUR GRIP FOR GREATER OR LESSER DISTANCES.*

NOTE: *GENERALLY, THE POINT-FIRST METHOD IS USED FOR VERY CLOSE RANGE, THE BASIC THROW FOR INTERMEDIATE RANGE AND THE OVERHEAD BLADE-HELD METHOD FOR EXTREME DISTANCE.*

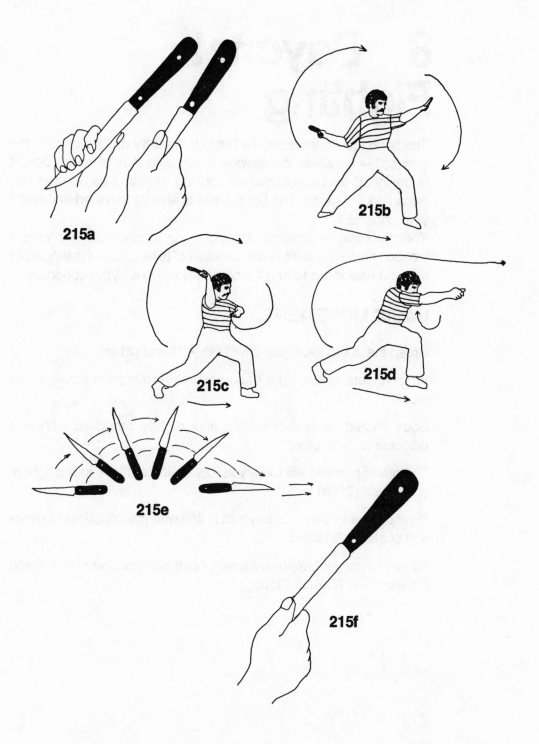

215a

215b

215c

215d

215e

215f

8 Bayonet Fighting

The bayonet is considered by the U.S. Infantry as "the spirit of the offense" — *however, the bayonet is strictly a defensive weapon.* It is designed for use only when you are attacked before you can reload your weapon. The best advise is always to reload and shoot your opponent.

The objective of bayonet fighting is: to knock your opponent's weapon aside (remember the principle of leverage — the longer his rifle, the easier it is to turn his blade aside); to kill your opponent.

BASIC MOVEMENT:

Grasp the upper handguard with the left hand (**216a**).

Wrap fingers of the right hand securely around the small of the stock.

Body should be well-balanced and slightly crouched with feet diagonal to each other.

The guard position will force your opponent to attack to the right of your blade (**216b**).

Pivot body and turn your bayonet in line with your opponent's direction of attack (**216c**).

As you knock your opponent's weapon, thrust your blade in line with his attack — TO KILL (**216d**).

216a

216b

216c

216d

THE HAND CUT:

If opponent hesitates in his attack or attempts to spar, slice his hand (**217**).

COUNTER TO HEAD-ON ATTACK:

Meet attack from guard position (**218a**).

As opponent rushes into range, knock his weapon aside while moving your body to the left with the right (rear) leg (**218b**).

Maintain balance with the left (leading) leg moving body out of line of opponent's attack (**218c**).

Thrust your bayonet into opponent's body as it passes (**218d**).

217

218a

218b

218c

218d

LOCKED WEAPONS:

If you are unsuccessful in knocking your opponent's weapon aside and your weapons become locked (**219a**), whip your blade back into his temple or neck (**219b**).

BASIC BUTT STROKE:

If your opponent blocks your thrust (**220a**), drive your rifle butt low into his groin (**220b**).

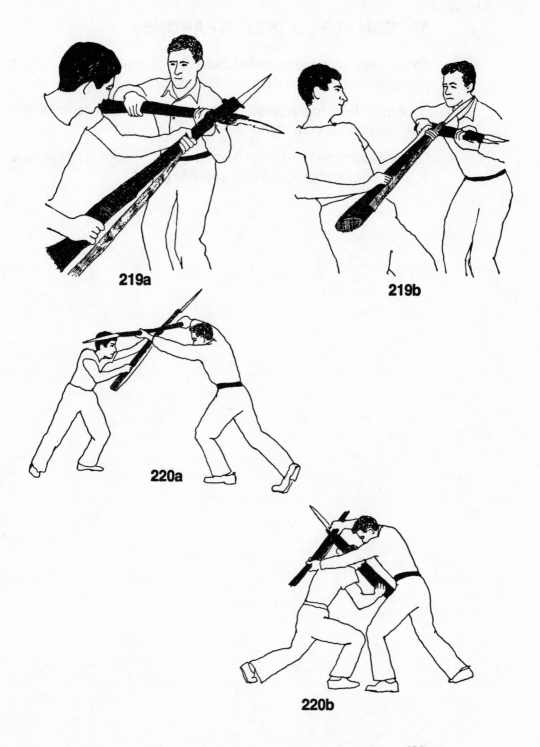

219a

219b

220a

220b

ALTERNATE LOCKED WEAPONS:

Should your weapons become locked (**221a**) remove pressure from your opponent's blade and let it slide by (**221b**).

Once his blade has passed, whip your own blade around into a head slash or arm cut (**221c**).

Follow through on the cut and drop down into position for a vigorous thrust into your opponent's exposed side (**221d**).

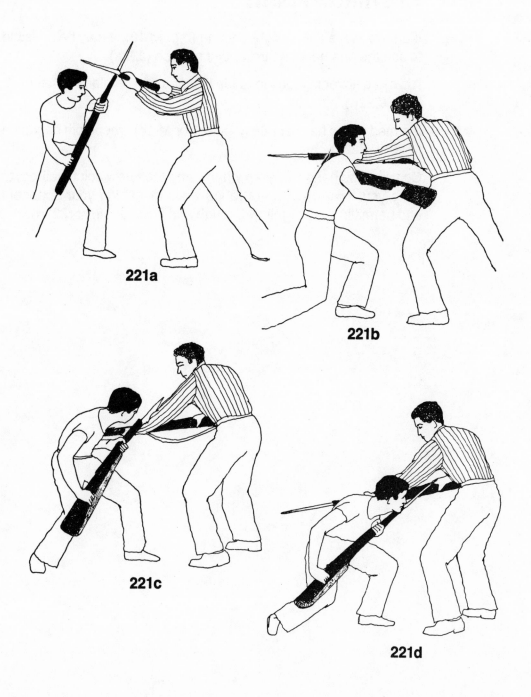

221a

221b

221c

221d

THE THROW POINT:

If armed with a light-weight carbine (e.g. M-16), it may be possible to use the one-handed throw point method (**222a**).

It is more advantageous to guide the direction of attack with the left hand (**222b**).

If armed with a heavier rifle (e.g. M-1 or M-14), keep both hands on the rifle (**222c**).

Consider the hand cut, even when using the throw point method, to keep your own body out-of-range while disarming your opponent and permitting you to follow through and finish the fight (**222d**).

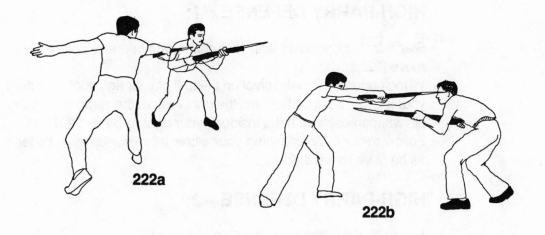

222a

222b

222c

222d

HIGH-PARRY DEFENSE #1:

Stand facing opponent with feet comfortably spread and ready to move (**223a**).

When opponent thrusts, pivot on the ball of your right foot, dropping your left foot back on line with the right foot; at the same time, parry his weapon aside with the inside of your right forearm (**223b**).

Follow through by smashing your elbow into your opponent's face as he drive forward (**223c**).

HIGH-PARRY DEFENSE #2:

Start with the same basic position (#1 above).

When opponent thrusts, pivot on the ball of your right foot, and drop left foot back on line with it; at the same time, parry your opponent's weapon aside with the inside of your right forearm (**224a**).

Thrust up with your left hand and grasp your opponent's hand and the upper hand guard of your opponent's rifle, locking his hand to the weapon (**224b**).

Step across with your right foot to block his right leg; at the same time, bring down your right arm across his left arm and grasp the receiver of his rifle with your right hand (**224c**).

Twist your body in one continuous motion to your left, throwing your opponent over your right leg (**224d**).

Follow through and finish him off with his own weapon (**224e**).

223a

223b

223c

224a

224b

224c

224d

224e

9 Stick Fighting

THE LONG STICK TECHNIQUE:

Grasp the stick approximately 4 inches from the bottom with the long portion directed at your opponent (**225**).
There are many uses for this technique

      A. (**226a**).

      B. (**226b**).

      C. (**226c**).

      D. (**226d**).

      E. (**226e**).

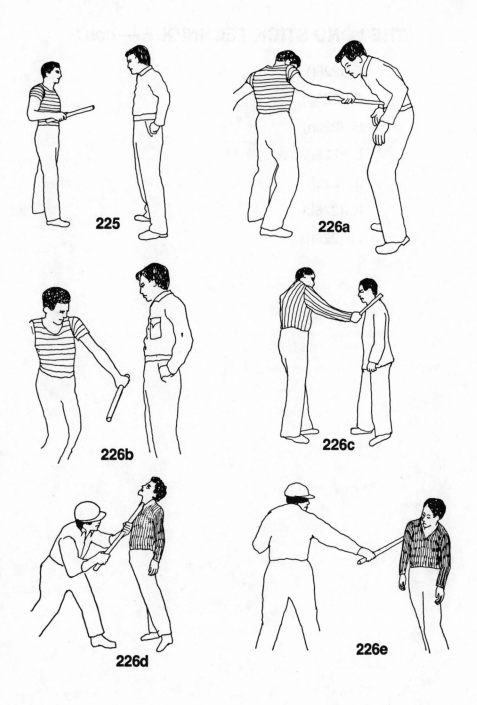

225

226a

226b

226c

226d

226e

THE LONG STICK TECHNIQUE — *con't.:*

F. (226f).

G. (226g).

H. (226h).

I. (226i).

J. (226j).

K. (226k).

L. (226l).

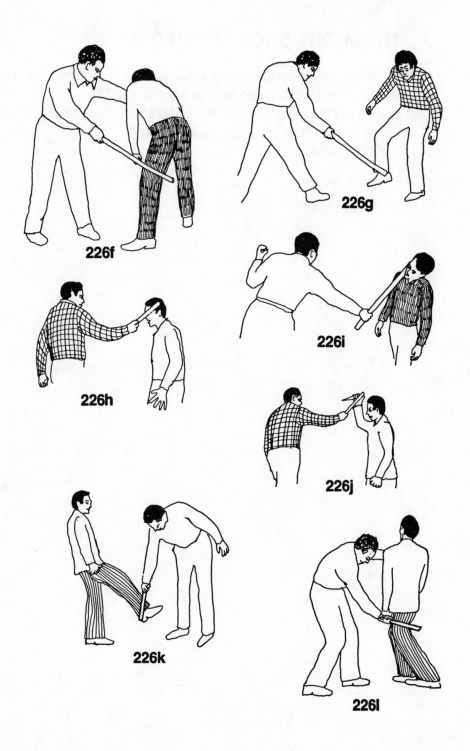

226f

226g

226h

226i

226j

226k

226l

THE SHORT STICK TECHNIQUE:

Grasp the stick approximately 4 inches from the forward end keeping the short end directed at your opponent **(227)**.

The short stick is used much the same as the Jawara or judo stick. Some examples of the short stick in action:

    A. **(228a)**.

    B. **(228b)**.

    C. **(228c)**.

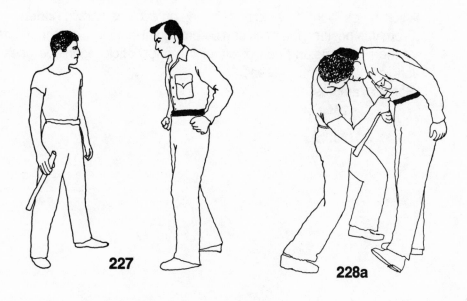

227

228a

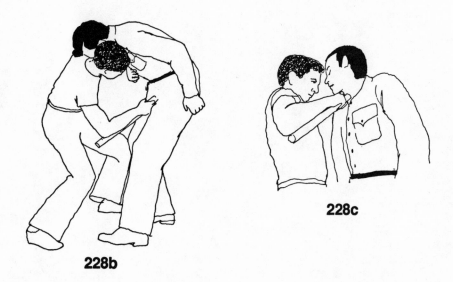

228b

228c

CLOSED OR HIDDEN STICK TECHNIQUE:

Stick is held behind back, both hands on stick as shown (**229a**).
From this position the stick can be brought into action on either side
of the body, making use of either the short stick technique or the
long stick technique (**229b**).
Some examples:

     A. (**230a**).

     B. (**230b**).

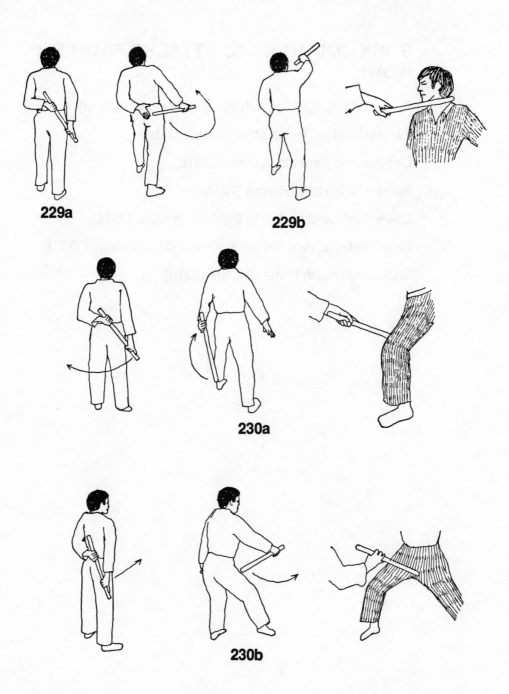

229a

229b

230a

230b

STICK COUNTERS TO ATTACKS FROM THE REAR:

Extended backhand smash to the wrist or arm (**231a**).

Two-handed jab to the solar plexus (**231b**).

One-handed thrust to the groin (**231c**).

Backhand jab to the throat (**231d**).

Lower backhand smash to the thigh or knee (**231e**).

Backhand smash to the neck, side of skull or temple (**231f**).

Backhand smash to the rib cage (**231g**).

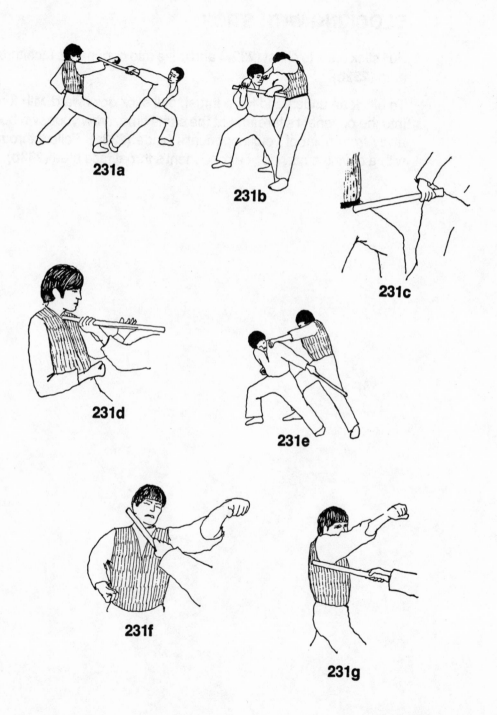

231a

231b

231c

231d

231e

231f

231g

BLOCKING WITH STICK:

Pull stick back to chest (**232a**) and drive into opponent's face/throat area (**232b**).

To block an underhand knife thrust, pull stick downward with force into the opponent's forearm; at the same time, draw your own body away from point of your opponent's blade (**233a**). Follow through with a driving smash to your opponent's throat/face area (**233b**).

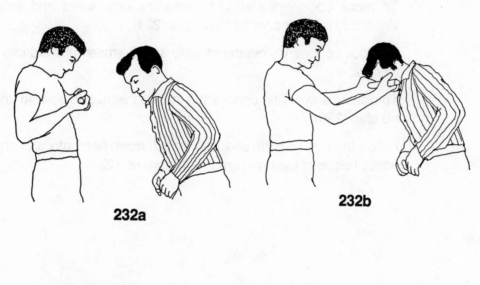

232a

232b

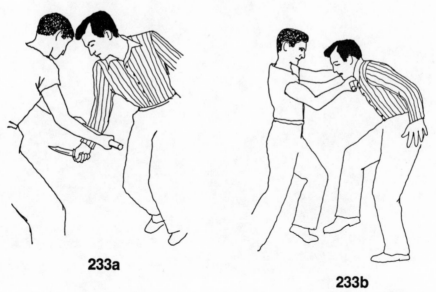

233a

233b

BLOCKING WITH STICK — *con't.:*

To block opponent's kick, thrust stick downward and smash vigorously into opponent's shin bone (**234**).

To block opponent's overhand knife thrust, smash upward into his wrist (**235**).

To disable a wrestling opponent, smash forward and upward under his chin (**236**).

Follow through with the stick and smash down hard into your opponent's bridge of the nose area — this will *kill* (**237**).

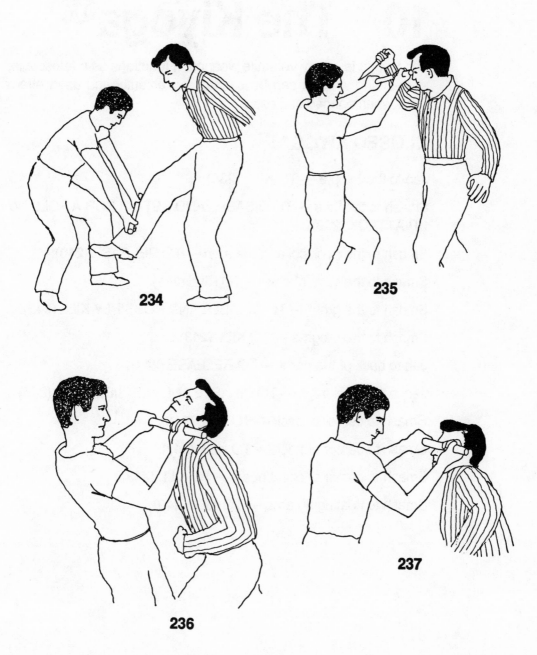

234

235

236

237

10   The Kiyoga™

The kiyoga is a very versatile weapon. It functions as a telescopic, steel-spring whip. It can be carried conveniently and used effectively when opened or closed.

CLOSED KIYOGA:

Jab to the temple — TO KILL **(238)**.

Smash to the face — TO DISABLE AND SET-UP FOR A FOLLOW UP ATTACK **(239)**.

Smash to the neck/collar bone area — TO RELEASE **(240)**.

Smash to the solar plexus — TO KILL **(241)**.

Smash to the groin — TO DISABLE AND POSSIBLY KILL **(242)**.

Smash to the bregma — TO KILL **(243)**.

Jab to back of the hand — TO RELEASE **(244)**.

Jab to the inner thigh — TO DISABLE AND POSSIBLY KILL **(245)**.

Smash to center of back — TO KILL **(246)**.

Smash to center of neck — TO KILL **(247)**.

Smash to center of chest/heart — TO KILL **(248)**.

Smash to floating rib area — TO KILL **(249)**.

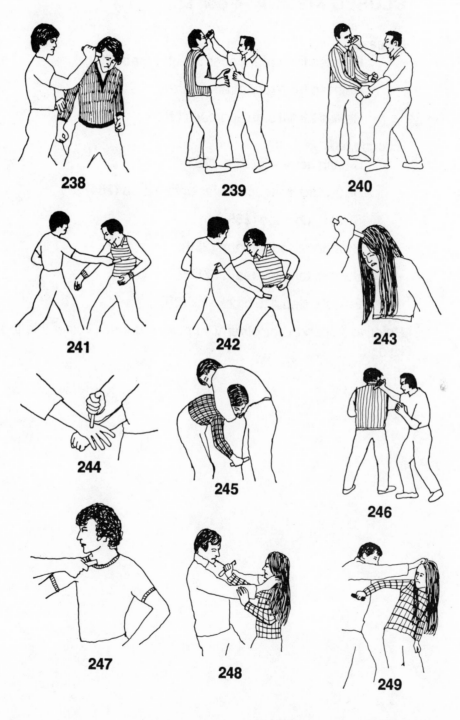

238

239

240

241

242

243

244

245

246

247

248

249

CLOSED KIYOGA — *con't.:*

Releases:

Release from rear under-the-arm grab **(250)**.

Release from rear strangle **(251)**.

Release from side approach **(252)**.

Extended Kiyoga:

Smash across forearm **(253)**.

Backward swat across face/nose area **(254)**.

Swat to rib cage **(255)**.

Swat to raised forearm **(256)**.

Swat to temple area **(257)**.

Smash to shin to block kick **(258)**.

Refer to Appendix for other vital points that are vulnerable to the kiyoga.

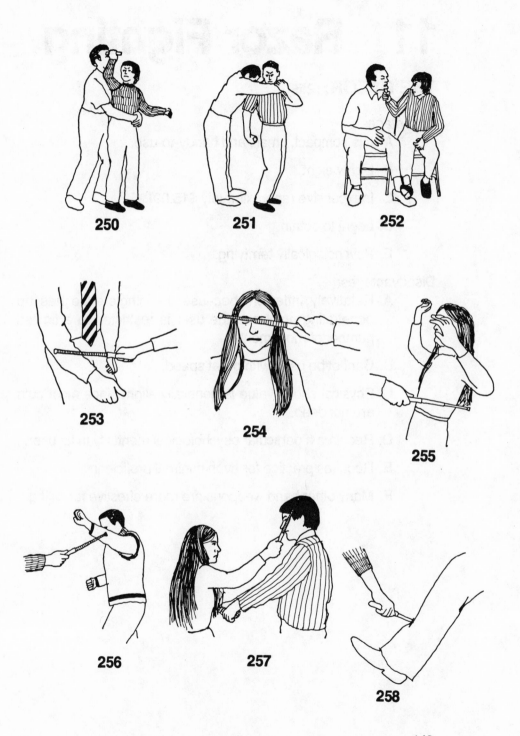

250

251

252

253

254

255

256

257

258

11 Razor Fighting

THE RAZOR: (259)

Advantages:
- A. It is compact, small, and handy-to-use.

- B. Lightweight.

- C. Inexpensive (approximately $15.00).

- D. Legal to obtain.

- E. Psychologically terrifying.

Disadvantages:
- A. Relatively inflexible because the single-edge has no penetrating point and the user is restricted to a limited number of movements.

- B. Cannot be used with great speed.

- C. Physical shock value is generally slight since most cuts are not deep.

- D. Requires a particular psychological mentality in its user.

- E. Requires practice for even minimal proficiency.

- F. Many other hand weapons are more effective for killing.

259

CARRY, GRIP, STANCE:

Carry in the front pocket of pants for easy accessibility (**260**). When jacket or topcoat is worn, carry in the most easily accessible pocket (**261**).

Avoid fance paraphanalia such as behind-the-neck sheaths, sleeve sheaths, etc.

Locked-Out-Grip (**262**) is fast and suitable for slashing attacks.

Fold-Over-Grip (**263**) is suitable for power slashes and will effect the most fatal slashes.

Practice use from natural stance (**264**).

Maintain balance; never let feet cross, always shuffle forward, backward, sideward — *shuffle, shuffle, shuffle, shuffle, slash.*

Practice until your entire body moves as one unit and the slash becomes merely an extension of the total move — *practice.*

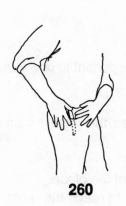

260

261

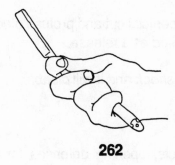

262

263

264

VITAL TARGET POINTS:

1. Throat (**265**):

    Kill with a deep slash.

    A feint to the throat will force opponent to cover-up providing opening for low kick.

2. Side of Neck (**266**):

    A deep slash KILLS if it slices the jugular vein or carotid artery.

3. Eyes (**267**):

    Attack with sharpened corner of the blade.

    If penetration is deep enough to reach the brain, *death* will result.

    A slashing attack *blinds.*

4. Inner Wrist (**268**):

    A slash will cause a superficial cut and profuse bleeding.

    A shash is effectively used as a release.

5. Groin (**269**):

    Effect is *psychological shock* and it will *disable.*

6. Achilles Tendon (**270**):

    Cripples instantly.

7. Face (**271**):

    Slashing attack distracts, opening defenses for alternate attack.

8. Alternate Points of Attack to entire Appendix section.

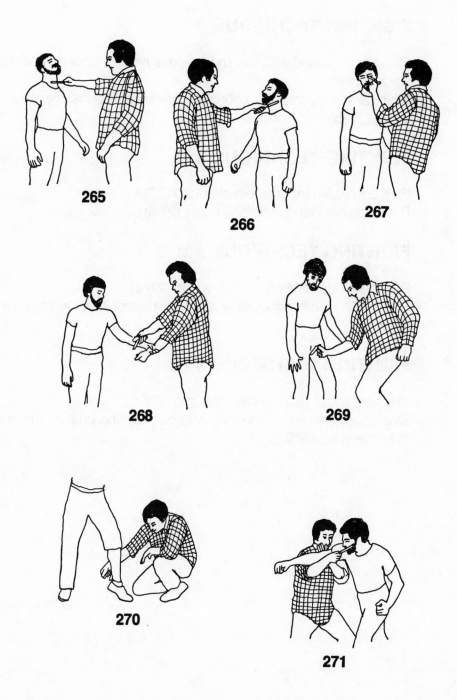

265

266

267

268

269

270

271

FIGHTING TECHNIQUE #1:

Stand in a relaxed attitude and prepare hidden razor for lock-out slash **(272a)**.

Whip razor suddenly and vigorously forward and across opponent's throat **(272b)**.

FIGHTING TECHNIQUE #2:

Prepare hidden razor in fold-over grip **(273a)**.

Drive upward into chin/lip/nose area **(273b)**.

FIGHTING TECHNIQUE #3:

Prepare hidden razor in fold-over grip **(274a)**.

Slash with a driving outside and downward thrust across face **(274b)**.

FIGHTING TECHNIQUE #4:

Prepare hidden razor in fold-over grip **(275a)**.

Slash suddenly and vigorously with outside and upward thrust to the outer neck **(275b)**.

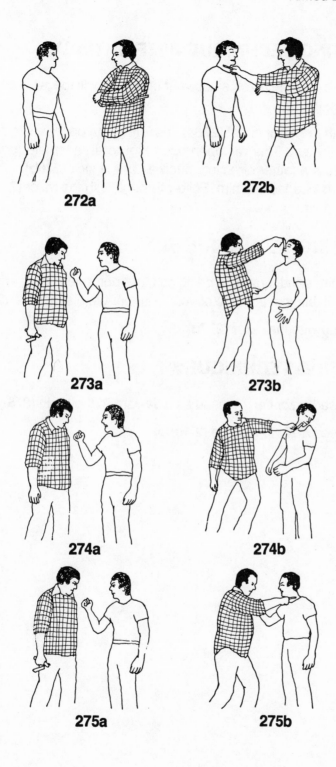

272a

272b

273a

273b

274a

274b

275a

275b

FIGHTING TECHNIQUE #5 (FEINTING):

Feint with only the razor, since your opponent will focus his concentration on it.

Feint with the razor thrust (**276a**) and force your opponent to defend against the cut. This will open open him to an alternate (primary) attack from another direction, such as a low kick (**276b**) or elbow (**276c**), to incapacitate him. Follow through with the razor (**276d**) to finish him off.

FIGHTING TECHNIQUE #6:

Throw dirt, sand, gravel, a brick, salt, pepper, a jacket, or anything else available into the face of your opponent to distract him (**277a**).

Follow-up with the razor (**277b**).

FIGHTING TECHNIQUE #7:

The closed razor can be used as a Jawara to the groin (**278a**).

Jab closed razor to the eye (**278b**).

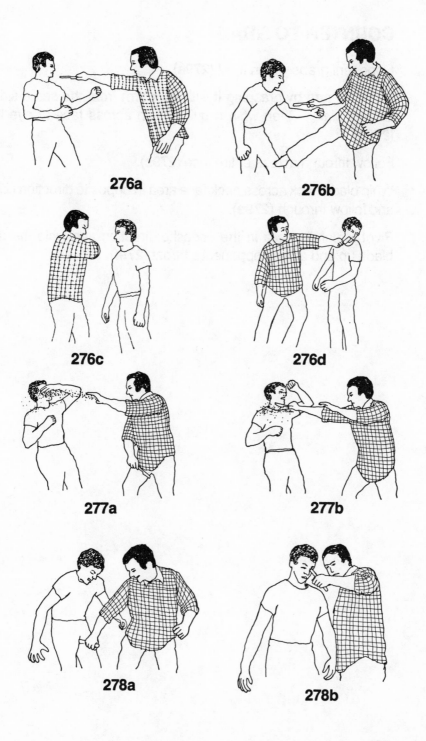

276a

276b

276c

276d

277a

277b

278a

278b

COUNTER TO GRAB:

Opponent grabs you in front (**279a**).

Block his arm by grasping it with your arm from the same side *to distract him* — then whip a quick slash across face at eye level (**279b**).

Follow through across entire face (**279c**).

Whip blade back across neck/face area in opposite direction (**279d**) and follow through (**279e**).

Pivot forcefully back in the opposite direction and whip the razor blade up and across opponent's throat (**279f**).

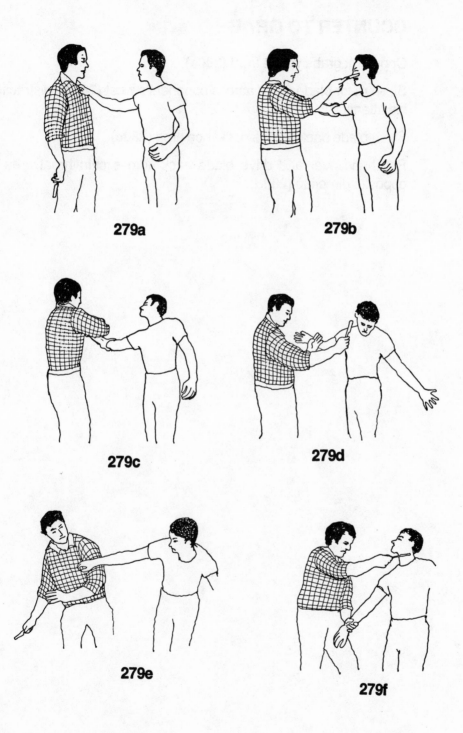

279a

279b

279c

279d

279e

279f

COUNTER TO GRAB:

Opponent grabs you in front (**280a**).

Slash razor blade down across opponent's wrist (**280b**), distracting his attention.

Slash blade back across neck/face area (**280c**).

Roll hand over and drive blade back across chin/throat area in opposite direction (**280d**).

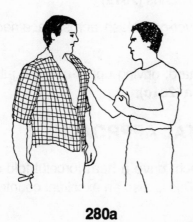

280a

280b

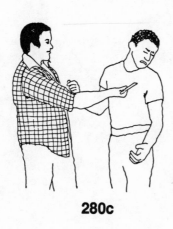

280c

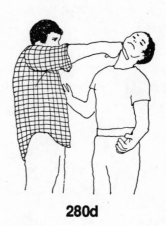

280d

COUNTER TO TWO-HAND GRAB:

Opponent grasp you with two hands (**281a**).

Whip a hard, driving, fold-over-grip slash across face/neck area (**281b**).

Go between his arms with hard, driving upper-cut using the fold-over-grip to the chin/face area (**281c**).

COUNTER TO FRONTAL APPROACH:

As opponent gets within reach, drive a hard forceful fold-out-grip slash to the groin (**282a**) — This is also an excellent counter to the two hand grab.

Follow through up the chest into the neck/chin/face area (**282b**).

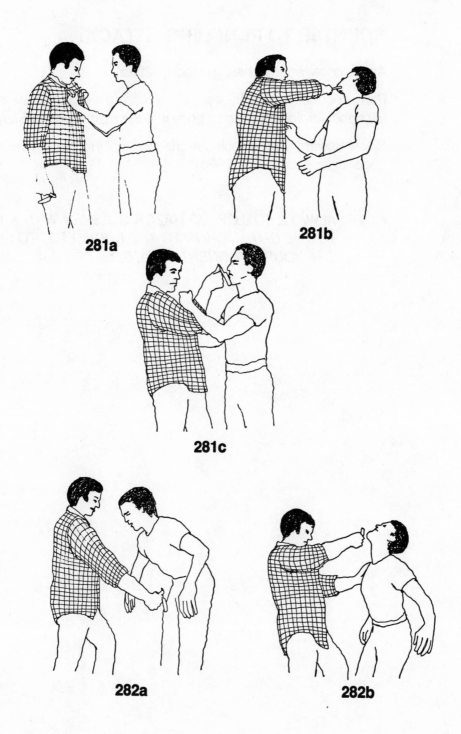

281a

281b

281c

282a

282b

COUNTER TO PUNCHING ATTACK:

As opponent approaches, get ready (**283a**).

Parry opponent's blow by stepping to outside and parrying with your left hand, forcing opponent's body into the razor's path (**283b**).

Slash upward with a lock-out-grip and rip the blade across the opponent's cheek/eyes (**283c**).

*NOTE: ALWAYS FOLLOW-UP RAZOR SLASHES WITH A KNEE TO THE GUT, A CHOP TO THE NECK, ETC., TO FINISH OFF YOUR OPPONENT (**284a, b, c**).*

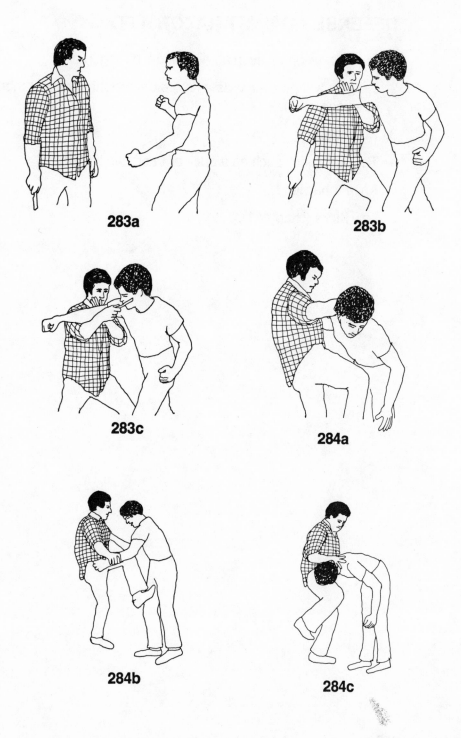

283a

283b

283c

284a

284b

284c

DEFENSE AGAINST RAZOR ATTACK:

1. Superior weapon, such as a shotgun, handgun or rifle.

2. Lengthy weapon, such as a lead pipe, weighted cane, umbrella or kiyoga (**285**).

3. Chair (**286**).

4. Thrown object, such as a brick or trash can lid (**287**).

5. Knife (**chapter 7**).

6. Low Kicks (chapter 1).

285

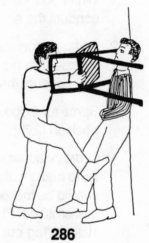

286

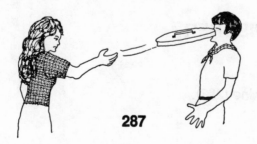

287

12 Special Military Situations

METHODS OF PRISONER SEARCH

1. Order prisoner to stand with legs so wide apart that it is impossible to move either foot off ground without losing his balance. Order prisoner to put his hands on top of head and remain silent. While you keep him covered from the rear with your weapon, conduct the search with your free hand (**288**).

2. Order prisoner to stretch out face down on ground; press rifle's muzzle into his back and keep your finger on the trigger while you conduct the search with your free hand (**289**).

3. Same as 2 above, except order prisoner to assume the kneeling position (**290**).

4. Order prisoner to lean against a wall with his feet so far from wall as to make it almost impossible to hold position. Prisoner's arms should be locked on top of head, his elbows against wall and his feet crossed. Place your knee against his so that you are able to kick his leg out from him, if necessary. Keep him covered with your weapon from the rear while you conduct the search with your free hand (**291**).

GAGGING A PRISONER

1. With cloth (**292**).

2. With a stick and twine (**293**).

3. With tape (**294**).

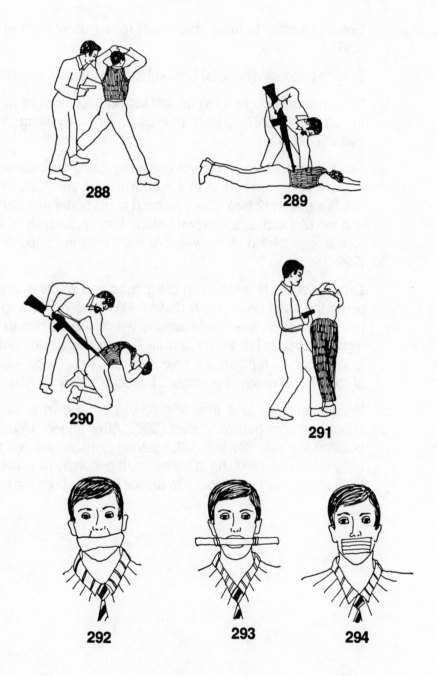

288

289

290

291

292

293

294

SECURING A PRISONER

Secure hand(s) to fixed object with rope (follow hitch in drawing) (**295**).

Secure prisoner's hand(s) behind his body using a belt (**296**).

Secure prisoner's hand(s) behind his body using light twine. First, tie his wrists (**297a**), then, strengthen bond by tying thumbs together (**297b**).

Secure prisoner to a chair with one arm around the back of the chair and the other arm behind him but not around the chair. First, tie his wrists together (**298a**). Then, tie each of his upper arms to the sides and top of the chair as shown (**298b**). Finally, tie both of his ankles to the legs of the chair, with his toes unable to touch the floor (**298c**).

Order prisoner face-down on the ground and tie his wrists together using the fixed-object hitch (**299a**). Run long end of rope around prisoner's neck, then once around wrists. Force him to bend his legs up against his thighs and tie legs in position by passing the long end of the rope around ankles as required. Tie off, keeping end of rope out of reach of prisoner's hands or mouth (**299b**).

Secure prisoner to a tree or pole using his own body. Prisoner should be attached as shown (**300**). After fifteen minutes in this position the prisoner will suffer severe cramps and will throw his body backward resulting in his death. It generally requires two men to lift a prisoner high enough to unlock his legs from the pole.

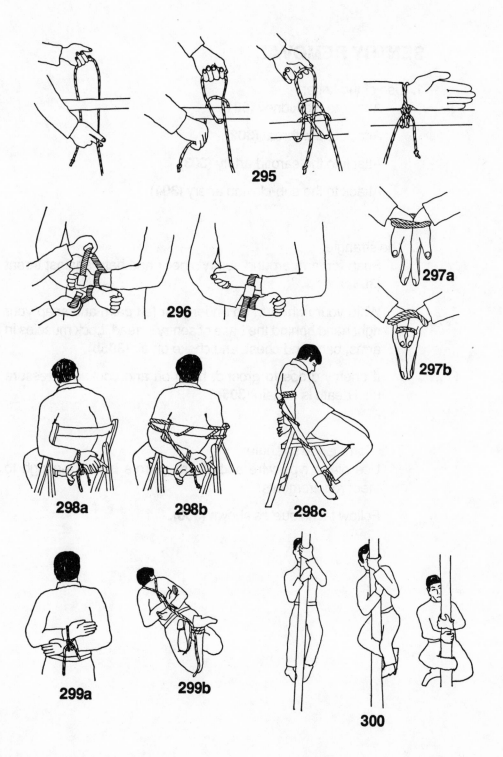

295

296

297a

297b

298a   **298b**   **298c**

299a   **299b**

300

SENTRY REMOVAL

1. Use of the knife:

    Attack to the kidney (**301**).

    Attack to the throat (**302**).

    Attack to the carotid artery (**303**).

    Attack to the sub-clavian artery (**304**).

2. The strangle:

    Snap forearm around sentry's neck and hard against throat (**305a**).

    Whip your right arm up under your left palm and snap your right hand behind the base of sentry's head. Lock muscles in arms, back and chest, and choke off air (**305b**).

    If enemy drops to ground, hang on and continue pressure until death is certain (**305c**).

3. The Commando strangle:

    Use piano type wire and insure garrote is long enough to meet requirements.

    Follow technique as shown (**306**).

301

302

303

304

305a

305b

305c

306

SENTRY REMOVAL — *con't.:*

4. Hatchet to medulla (**307**).

5. Long sword decapitation (**308**).

6. Entrenching tool to medulla or spine (**309**).

7. Rifle butt to spine, generally renders unconsciousness but does not kill (**310**).

8. Rifle muzzle to spine (**311**).

9. Helmet to medulla (**312**).

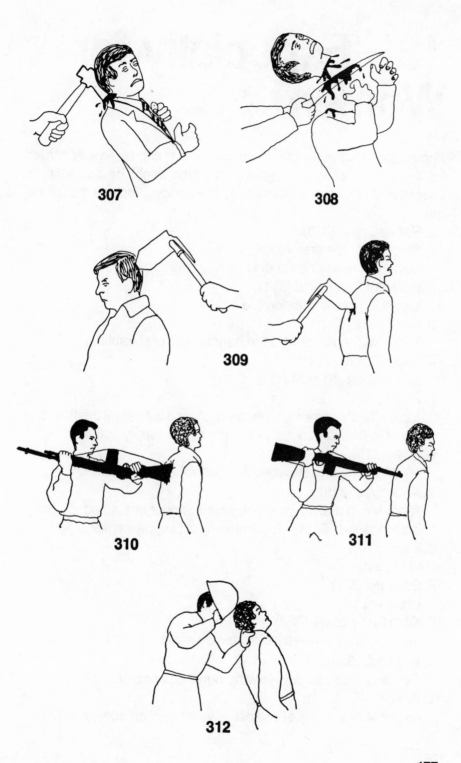

307

308

309

310

311

312

13 Especially for Women

Items commonly available to women, which can be legally carried on the person or in the purse and which might be successfully utilized and anti-rape and anti-assault weapons, include the following:

1. Rattail Comb (**313**):
   Steel types are preferable.
   Generally available through beauty supply centers.
2. Ballpoint Pen/Pencil (**314**):
   Metallic types are preferable.
3. Nail File (**315**):
   Types with bone or wooden handles are preferable.
4. Letter Openers (**316**):
   Metal types are preferable.
5. Hairbrush (**317**):
   Most effective types should be equipped with steel bristles. Obtainable through animal grooming or pet supply outlets.
6. Nails (**318**):
   30-60 penny is preferable. An extremely effective dirk.
7. Art Knives (**319**):
   Available in many types from thumb-finger controlled to spring blade loaded. Obtainable from any art supply center.
8. Keys (**320**):
   In the fist.
9. Scissors (**321**):
   In the fist.
10. Knife Sharpeners (**322**):
    Various types are available. Use as a dirk.
11. Key Club (**323**):
    Can be utilized as dirk, jawara, nunchuck or blackjack.
12. Artist Scribe (**324**):
    As lethal as a medical scalpel. Available at art supply centers.

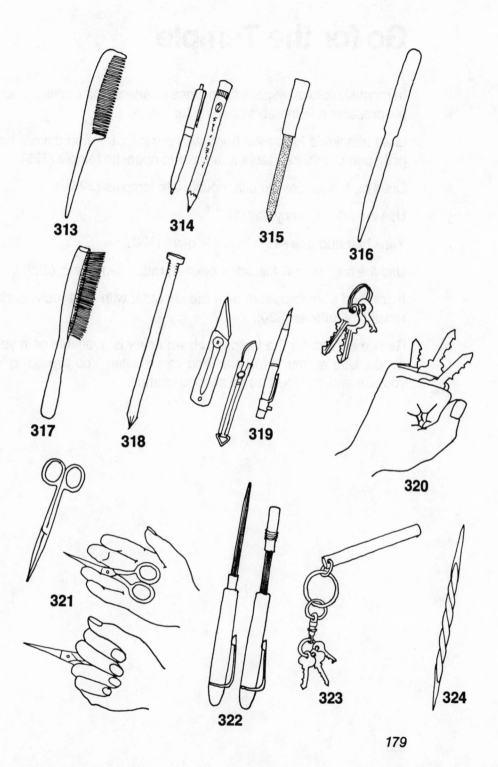

313

314

315

316

317

318

319

320

321

322

323

324

Go for the Temple

In most situations, especially in close quarters, the attacker's temple presents a vulnerable opening for attack.

Grab attacker's hair, twist head with a hard yank and drive a ball-point pen or other suitable weapon into opposite temple (**325**).

Drive both knuckles simultaneously into temples (**326**).

Use the 30-60 penny nail (**327**).

Yank hair and use single/knuckle drive (**328**).

Use the fingers, nail file, letter opener, rattail comb, etc. (**329**).

If grabbed from rear, stab over the shoulder with hairbrush handle, rattail or whatever (**330**).

Remember, go for the temple with whatever is available or in your hands. Use as much force as you can muster. You are going for your life and there will be no second chance.

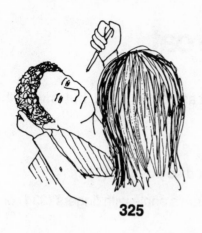

325

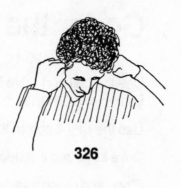

326

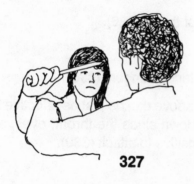

327

328

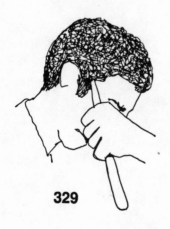

329

330

Go for the Throat

Use the nail and drive for the base of the throat, but drive with all of your might (**331**).

Use the rattail comb (**332**).

Drive keys into the neck as hard as possible (**333**).

Pinch and crush attacker's Adam's apple with fingers (**334**) or chop with the edge-of-the-hand.

Smash your forearm across attacker's Adam's apple (**335**).

Drive your knuckles to base of throat (**336**).

Stab with scissors (**337**).

Drive into throat with your extended fingers (**338**).

Keep in mind that any of the above can be just as effective from on your back while being held down since the throat, eyes, etc., are extremely vulnerable and sensitive to attack (**339**).

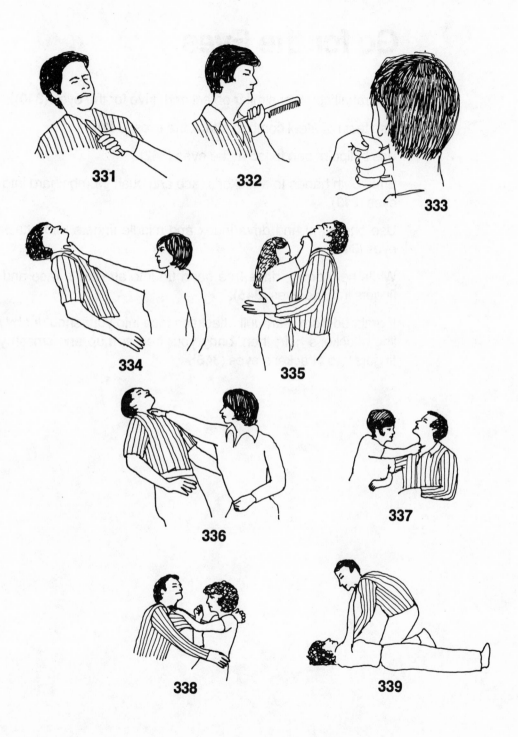

331

332

333

334

335

336

337

338

339

Go for the Eyes

Use rattail comb or similar object and drive for the eyes (**340**).

Use teeth of steel comb to attack the eyes (**341**).

Use ballpoint pen to jab at the eyes (**342**).

Bring both hands to attacker's face and push thumbs hard into the eyes (**343**).

Use one hand and drive index and middle fingers into attacker's eyes (**344**).

While held down, drive free hand up into attacker's face and jab fingers into the eyes (**345**).

If grabbed from rear, pull attacker's face into your shoulder by pulling attacker's hair; then, bring your free arm up and smash your fingers into attacker's eyes (**346**).

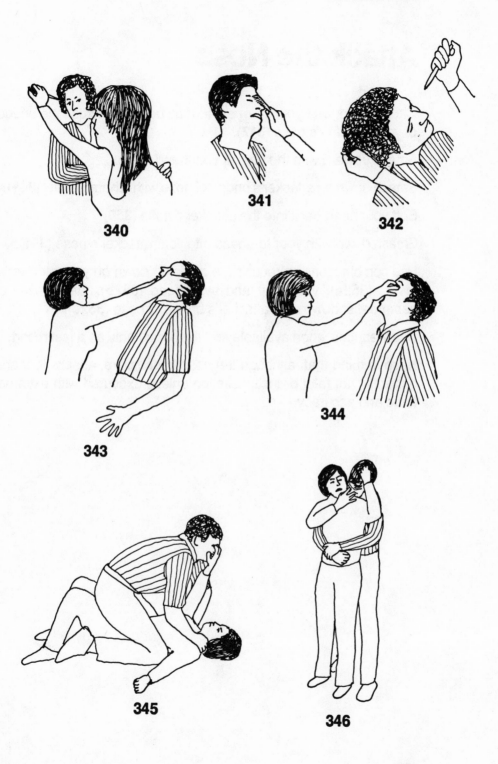

340

341

342

343

344

345

346

Attack the Nose

Chop the edge of your palm as hard as possible across the bridge of your attacker's nose (**347**).

Smash upward with the heel of your hand (**348**).

Smash down on attacker's bridge of nose with a hammer-fist (**349**).

Butt your head back into the attacker's nose (**350**).

Smash down with your forehead into your attacker's nose (**351**).

Use combinations as required, e.g. stomp down on your attacker's instep (**352a**), yank hair and twist head (**352b**), then smash a hammer-fist down onto attacker's bridge of nose (**352c**).

Use weapons when available and the hands only as a last resort.

Keep in mind that, although the nose is sensitive, attacks to it are generally not fatal or incapacitating unless executed with extreme force and accuracy.

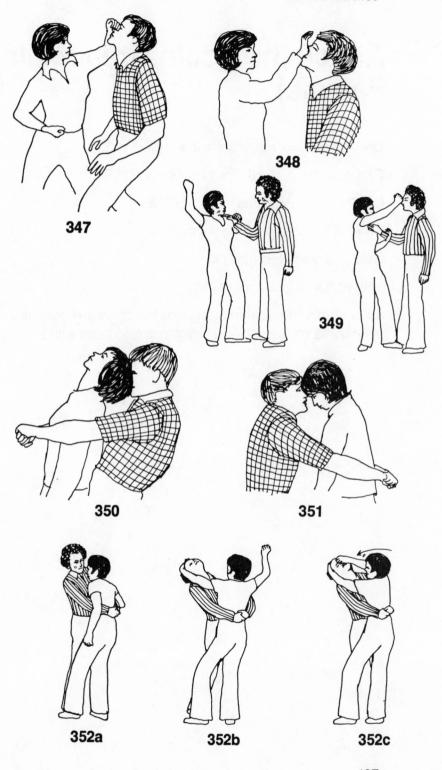

347

348

349

350

351

352a

352b

352c

Attack the Groin Area (Male or Female)

Drive a letter opener or knife to the groin (**353**).

Give a back thrust with the rattail comb (**354**).

Use the hammer-fist as required (**355**).

Chop with the edge of the palm (**356**).

Grab and crush testicles (**357**).

Stab with a ballpoint pen (**358**).

Keep in mind that attack's against the groin are generally not as effective as old wives' tales indicate unless done with a weapon.

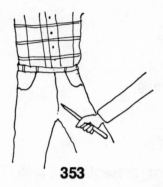

353

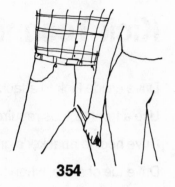

354

355

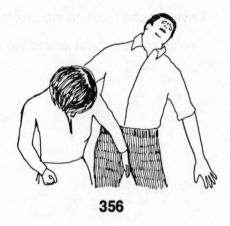

356

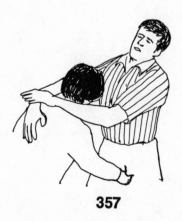

357

358

Kick Techniques

Drive a side kick to attacker's knee **(359)**.

Use a front kick as required **(360)**.

Drive heel to attacker's groin **(361)**.

Drive toe of shoe, when the opportunity presents itself **(362)**.

Smash a side kick into the solar plexus **(363)**.

Smash the knee **(364)**.

Drive leg and foot into attacker's crotch **(365)**.

Don't forget the back kick to the knee, when necessary **(366)**.

359

360

361

362

363

364

365

366

Attack the Stomach

Drive an elbow into side of attacker's rib cage (**367**).

Drive elbow straight back into attacker's guts (**368**).

Use your fist (**369**).

Smash fist into attacker's floating rib (**370**).

Smash the heel of your palm into the attacker's solar plexus (**371**).

Make use of a weapon whenever possible. This means that you should be prepared and have one in your hand and ready; you may not have time to get one out of your purse. HAVE IT READY (**372**).

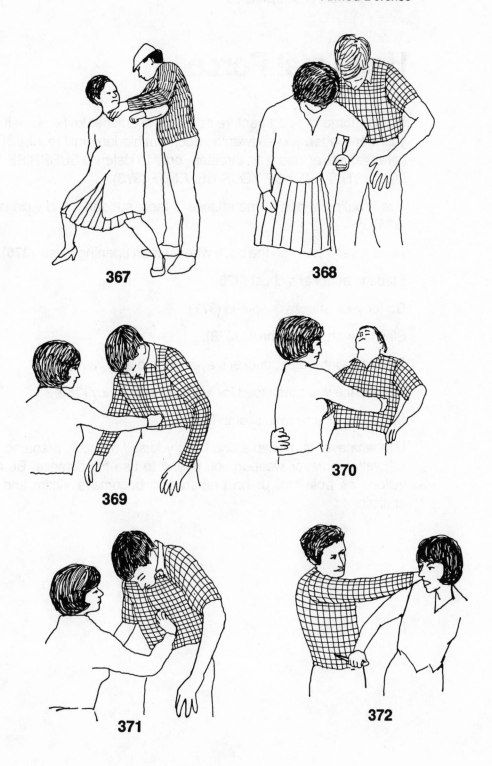

367

368

369

370

371

372

Use Total Force

In your home or apartment, remember the butcher knife. Have it in your hand when you answer the door, but hidden, until required for defense. Never use it to threaten, only to defend. SURPRISE IS MORE THAN 50% OF YOUR DEFENSE (**373**).

Use a ballpoint pen to the attacker's face, suddenly and viciously (**374**).

Drive a large nail into the body wherever an opening exists (**375**).

Stab the attacker's chest (**376**).

Go for your attacker's spleen (**377**).

Slash the attacker's throat (**378**).

Drive a nail through attacker's eye and into the brain (**379**).

Use the file you purchased for just this emergency (**380**).

Make use of your rattail comb (**381**).

Use whatever is available and keep yourself mentally prepared to kill, with whatever weapon you intend to use for defense. Be as vicious as possible, or be prepared to become a victim and a statistic.

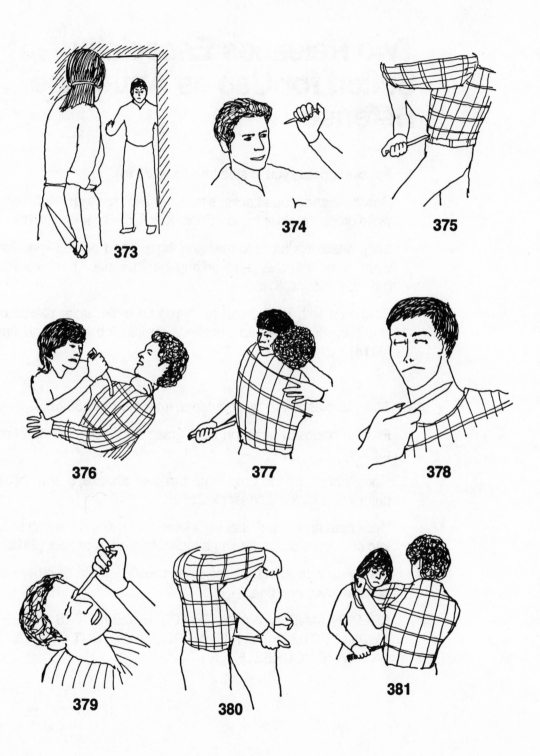

373

374

375

376

377

378

379

380

381

Two Releases Especially Suited for Use as Anti-Rape Defense

1. Attacker grasps you in side headlock (**381a**).

   Reach up and grab attacker's hair or grasp chin with inside palm while dropping other hand behind attacker near knee (**381b**).

   Snap attacker's head to rear and thrust hand behind knee forward lifting attacker and driving him/her over backward to ground or floor (**381c**).

   Follow up with heel crush to attacker's groin, solar plexus or chest, or drive toe into attacker's temple, rib cage, and flee (**381d**).

2. Attacker grasps you by shoulders, from the rear (**382a**).

   Pivot in opposite direction from grasp and block with forearm (**382b**).

   Complete pivot, and drop your arm over attacker's arm; thrust palm into attacker's chest (**382c**).

   Hook near leg behind attacker's knee continuing drive with palm into attacker's chest, forcing attacker to ground or floor (**382d**).

   Follow up with attack by toe to attacker's temple or other vulnerable area, and flee.

   KEEP IN MIND ALWAYS, THAT THE OBJECT IS TO GET AWAY. DESTROY OR KILL AS REQUIRED, BUT GET AWAY AND SAVE YOURSELF.

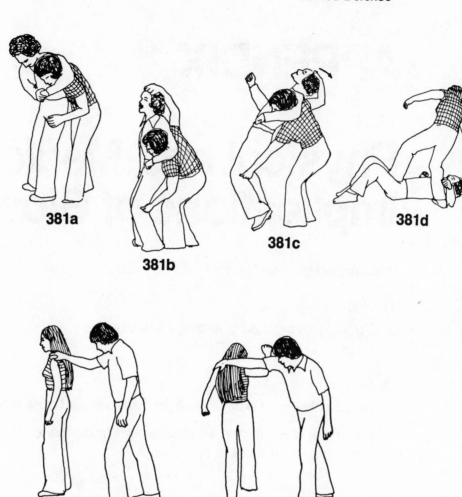

381a

381b

381c

381d

382a

382b

382c

382d

APPENDIX

Physical and Medical Implications of Blows

Vital areas of the head (**A-1**):

1) Hair:

   Pulling, yanking, and/or tearing causes pain.

2) Bregma:

   (Point at the top of skull where frontal and parietal bones meet.):

   A hammer blow with fist will dislocate the frontal bone, critically damaging motor areas of the brain (**A-2**).

3) Forehead:

   A sharp blow (**A-3**); ruptures the deep-lying blood vessels and blackens both eyes (**A-4**).

   Results in medium to severe contusion, depending on the number of blood vessels ruptured, UNCONSCIOUSNESS, COMA, and DEATH.

   Fractures the skull and/or frontal sinus (the cavity wall and into the brain followed by profuse bleeding through the nostrils, immediate UNCONSCIOUSNESS, COMA, and DEATH (**A-5**).

   Generally causes, in addition, whiplash, because of the sudden change of head position, followed by EXTREME PAIN and NECK STIFFNESS (**A-6**).

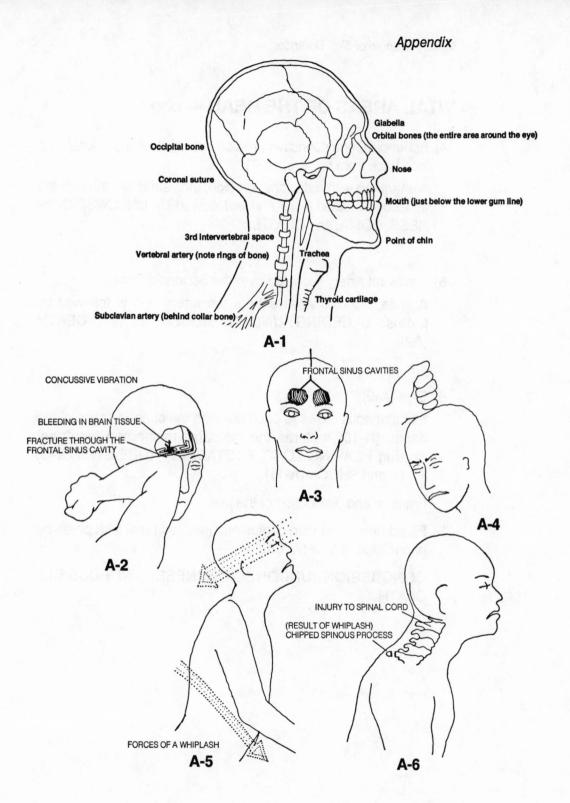

Glabella
Orbital bones (the entire area around the eye)
Occipital bone
Nose
Coronal suture
Mouth (just below the lower gum line)
3rd intervertebral space
Point of chin
Vertebral artery (note rings of bone)
Trachea
Thyroid cartilage
Subclavian artery (behind collar bone)

A-1

CONCUSSIVE VIBRATION

FRONTAL SINUS CAVITIES

BLEEDING IN BRAIN TISSUE

FRACTURE THROUGH THE
FRONTAL SINUS CAVITY

A-2

A-3

A-4

INJURY TO SPINAL CORD

(RESULT OF WHIPLASH)
CHIPPED SPINOUS PROCESS

FORCES OF A WHIPLASH

A-5

A-6

VITAL AREAS OF THE HEAD — *con't.:*

4) Sphenoid Bone (Concave area on side of skull approximately 1 inch back from the eye) **(A-7)**:

A sharp jab with a Jawara, knuckle, etc., smashes through the thin bone located here and is followed by UNCONSCIOUS-NESS, COMA, and DEATH.

5) Temporal Artery (Located over the Sphenoid Bone):

A knife or razor slash severs the artery and is followed by profuse BLEEDING, UNCONSCIOUSNESS, and DEATH **(A-8)**.

6) Ears **(A-9)**:

Simultaneous blows to each ear with the cupped palms of the hands **(A-10)** ruptures the tympanic membrane (eardrum) causing HEARING LOSS, EUSTACHIAN TUBE SWELLING, PAIN, and SHOCK **(A-11)**.

Fracture and dislocation of the jaw.

Facial nerve and vein contusions (bruised face) with paralysis of one side of face **(A-12)**.

CONCUSSION, UNCONSCIOUSNESS, and POSSIBLE DEATH.

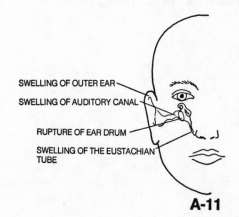

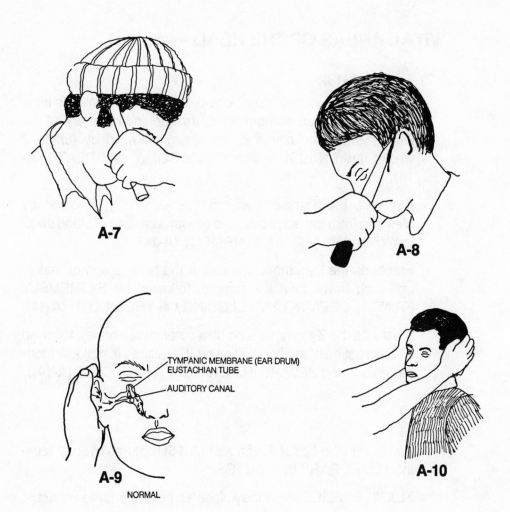

A-7

A-8

TYMPANIC MEMBRANE (EAR DRUM)
EUSTACHIAN TUBE

AUDITORY CANAL

A-9

NORMAL

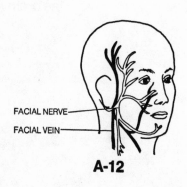

A-10

SWELLING OF OUTER EAR

SWELLING OF AUDITORY CANAL

RUPTURE OF EAR DRUM

SWELLING OF THE EUSTACHIAN
TUBE

A-11

FACIAL NERVE

FACIAL VEIN

A-12

VITAL AREAS OF THE HEAD — *con't.:*

7) Temple (**A-13**):

Jawara, ballpoint pen, rattail comb or back of fist knuckle blow fractures the area hemorrhaging the meningeal artery of the Dura (Membrane covering the brain) followed by (up to 2 weeks later) NAUSEA, VOMITING, COMA, and DEATH (**A-14**).

Ruptures the Tympanic Membrane (eardrum), followed by bleeding from the ear, nose, and mouth, vomiting of blood swallowed, and HEARING IMPAIRMENT (**A-14**).

Fractures the Zygomatic process, if the blow is approximately one inch lower than the temple, followed by EXTREMELY PAINFUL OPENING AND CLOSING OF THE MOUTH (**A-14**).

Fractures the Zygomatic arch (the outer cheek bone), followed by destruction of the floor of the orbit, resulting in diplopia (double vision) and SEVERE INJURY TO EYE MUSCLES (**A-14**).

8) Eye:

Attack with the tips of the fingers (**A-15**) ruptures eyeball causing TEMPORARY BLINDNESS.

TEARS EYELIDS since they close an instant prior to impact.

Results in DEATH if a sharp object is driven through and into the brain (**A-16**).

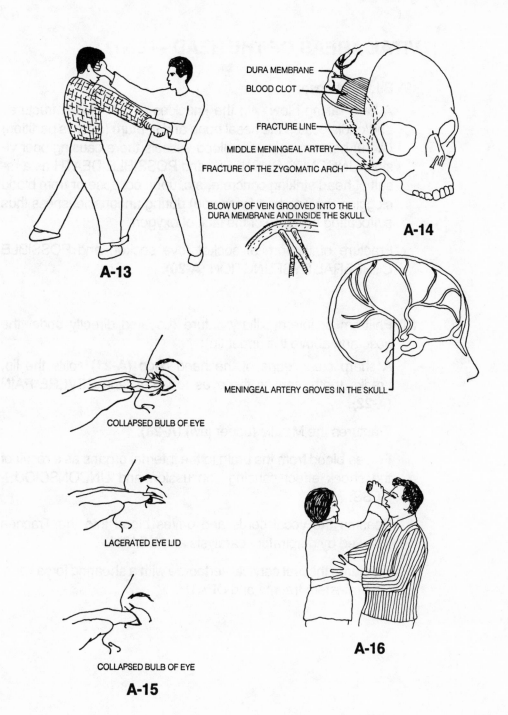

DURA MEMBRANE

BLOOD CLOT

FRACTURE LINE

MIDDLE MENINGEAL ARTERY

FRACTURE OF THE ZYGOMATIC ARCH

BLOW UP OF VEIN GROOVED INTO THE
DURA MEMBRANE AND INSIDE THE SKULL

A-14

A-13

MENINGEAL ARTERY GROVES IN THE SKULL

COLLAPSED BULB OF EYE

LACERATED EYE LID

COLLAPSED BULB OF EYE

A-15

A-16

VITAL AREAS OF THE HEAD — *con't.:*

9) Bridge of nose:

A hard raking blow with the knuckles (**A-17**) (**A-18**) fractures and/or dislocates the nasal bone and septum (nostrils partition) (**A-19**) hemorrhaging the blood vessels there causing poor vision, UNCONSCIOUSNESS, and POSSIBLE DEATH as a result of head striking concrete, etc. upon collapse or from blood clogging the Trachea (windpipe) during unconsciousness thus suffocating because of the lack of oxygen.

Fracture of the orbital socket (eye socket) and POSSIBLE CEREBRAL DYSFUNCTION (**A-20**).

10) Philtrum or intermaxillary suture (Located directly under the nose and above the upper lip):

A sharp clean edge of the hand chop (**A-21**) splits the lip, breaks teeth, causes the eyes to water, and SEVERE PAIN (**A-22**).

Fractures the Maxilla (upper jaw) (**A-23**).

Forces blood from the brain to the internal organs as a result of the shock effect causing concussion and UNCONSCIOUSNESS.

Spasms the vocal cords and drives blood into the Trachea followed by respiratory paralysis and DEATH.

Fractures the first cervical vertebrae with a shearing force causing brainstem trauma and DEATH.

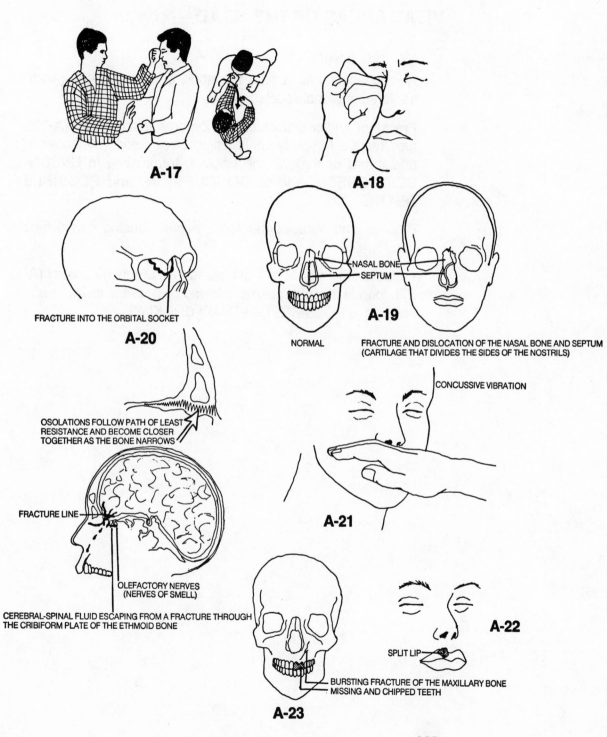

A-17

A-18

FRACTURE INTO THE ORBITAL SOCKET

A-20

NASAL BONE
SEPTUM

A-19

NORMAL   FRACTURE AND DISLOCATION OF THE NASAL BONE AND SEPTUM
(CARTILAGE THAT DIVIDES THE SIDES OF THE NOSTRILS)

OSOLATIONS FOLLOW PATH OF LEAST
RESISTANCE AND BECOME CLOSER
TOGETHER AS THE BONE NARROWS

CONCUSSIVE VIBRATION

FRACTURE LINE

OLEFACTORY NERVES
(NERVES OF SMELL)

CEREBRAL-SPINAL FLUID ESCAPING FROM A FRACTURE THROUGH
THE CRIBIFORM PLATE OF THE ETHMOID BONE

A-21

SPLIT LIP

A-22

BURSTING FRACTURE OF THE MAXILLARY BONE
MISSING AND CHIPPED TEETH

A-23

VITAL AREAS OF THE HEAD — *con't.:*

11) Mandible (jaw):

A simultaneous strike with the elbow and palm **(A-24) (A-25)** fractures and/or dislocates the jaw.

Fractures and/or dislocates the Zygoma (cheekbone) **(A-26)**, ruptures the Maxillary sinus letting blood flood into the sinus and throat or through the nostrils, terminating in UNCON-SCIOUSNESS, and/or CONCUSSION, and POSSIBLE DEATH.

Pinches and abrades the facial nerve, causing partial face paralysis.

Fractures the mandible and causes loss of tongue control **(A-27)**, tongue muscle spasms followed by possible tongue swallowing and POSSIBLE DEATH BY CHOKING.

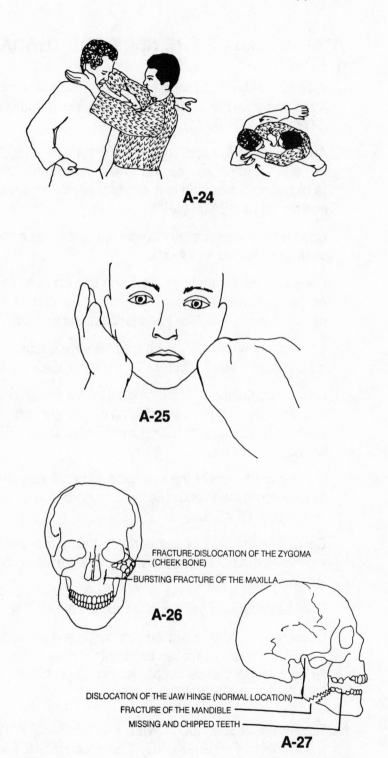

A-24

A-25

FRACTURE-DISLOCATION OF THE ZYGOMA
(CHEEK BONE)

BURSTING FRACTURE OF THE MAXILLA

A-26

DISLOCATION OF THE JAW HINGE (NORMAL LOCATION)

FRACTURE OF THE MANDIBLE

MISSING AND CHIPPED TEETH

A-27

VITAL AREAS OF THE NECK AND THROAT:

1) Throat:

An edge-of-the-hand chop to either the side or front (**A-28**) ruptures the internal jugular vein, causing hematoma and INSTANT DEATH (**A-29**).

As a result of the spasm of the vessel wall, the blood flow is restricted and causes carotid artery contusion and thrombosis (a blood clot), resulting in a cerebral anoxia (restricted oxygen) and stroke or DEATH (**A-30**).

Causes vertebratal artery contusion and/or laceration with results as noted above (**A-31**).

Causes a contusion in at least one branch of the vagus nerve which could result in lung and heart spasms followed by shortness of breath, irregular heart palpitations and DEATH.

Causes a contusion of the phrenic nerve, a sense of "having the wind knocked out," until RECOVERY or DEATH.

Causes contusion of the laryngeal nerve (vocal cord nerve), a branch of the vagus nerve, closing the vocal cords, blocking the trachea (windpipe) resulting in DEATH BY SUFFOCATION (**A-32**).

Causes contusion of the hypoglossal nerve resulting in loss of tongue control with possible swallowing of the tongue and thus POSSIBLE DEATH.

Causes hematoma of the carotid sheath (covers the internal jugular vein, carotid artery and vagus nerve) resulting in DEATH BY SUFFOCATION.

Causes fracture of the spinous process causing severe pain.

Causes a fracture to the thyroid cartilage (cricoid cartilage), if the blow is more frontal, activating the vocal cords and epiglottis, cutting off the air supply to the lungs followed by SLOW DEATH BY SUFFOCATION.

NOTE: ANY SINGLE BLOW WILL ENCOMPASS ANY COMBINATION OF THE ABOVE POSSIBLE RESULTS WITH ONE SINGLE RESULT ALWAYS APPARENT — DEATH. NEVER USE THIS BLOW IN TRAINING.

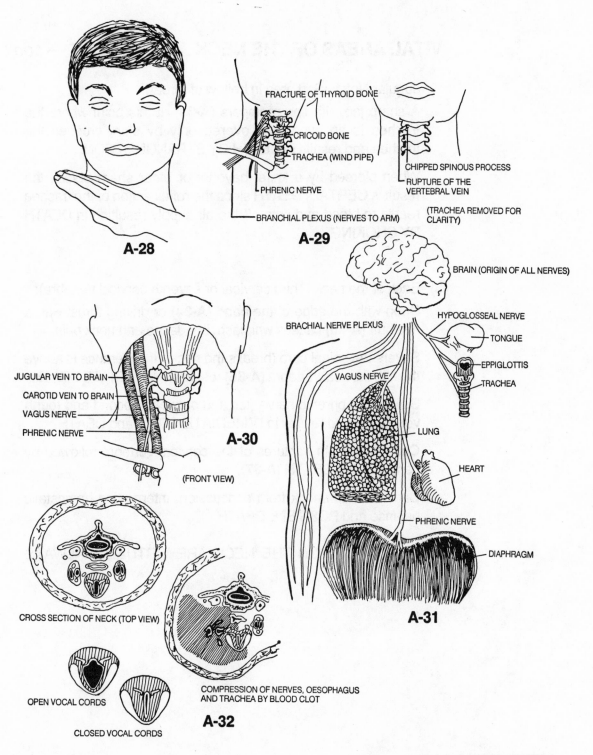

A-28

A-29

FRACTURE OF THYROID BONE

CRICOID BONE

TRACHEA (WIND PIPE)

PHRENIC NERVE

BRANCHIAL PLEXUS (NERVES TO ARM)

CHIPPED SPINOUS PROCESS

RUPTURE OF THE VERTEBRAL VEIN

(TRACHEA REMOVED FOR CLARITY)

BRAIN (ORIGIN OF ALL NERVES)

HYPOGLOSSEAL NERVE

TONGUE

EPPIGLOTTIS

TRACHEA

BRACHIAL NERVE PLEXUS

VAGUS NERVE

LUNG

HEART

PHRENIC NERVE

DIAPHRAGM

A-31

JUGULAR VEIN TO BRAIN

CAROTID VEIN TO BRAIN

VAGUS NERVE

PHRENIC NERVE

A-30

(FRONT VIEW)

CROSS SECTION OF NECK (TOP VIEW)

COMPRESSION OF NERVES, OESOPHAGUS AND TRACHEA BY BLOOD CLOT

OPEN VOCAL CORDS

CLOSED VOCAL CORDS

A-32

VITAL AREAS OF THE NECK AND THROAT — *con't.:*

2) Jugular Notch (Soft area in hollow of throat):

   A sharp jab with tips of fingers (**A-33**) at this point where the trachea is so exposed, covered only by skin, crushes the trachea and results in DEATH BY STRANGULATION.

   When pierced by a knife, bayonet or other sharp object, the result is CERTAIN DEATH since the reflex action of the trachea reacts to blood and cuts off the air supply resulting in DEATH BY CHOKING.

3) Back of the neck (Third cervical or seventh cervical vertebra):

   Chop with the edge of the hand (**A-34**) or driving thrust with a rifle butt (**A-35**) causes whiplash, headache and neck pain.

   Severs the spinal cord (breaks the neck). If severance is above the fifth cervical vertebra (**A-36**) results in IMMEDIATE DEATH.

   Severs the phrenic nerve (located between second and fourth vertebrae) and results in IMMEDIATE COMA and DEATH.

   Causes multiple fractures of the cervical vertebra followed by paralysis and DEATH (**A-37**).

   Causes brain shock from concussion, interrupting homostatic balance and POSSIBLE DEATH.

NOTE: ATTACKS ON THE NECK ARE VIRTUALLY ALWAYS FATAL!

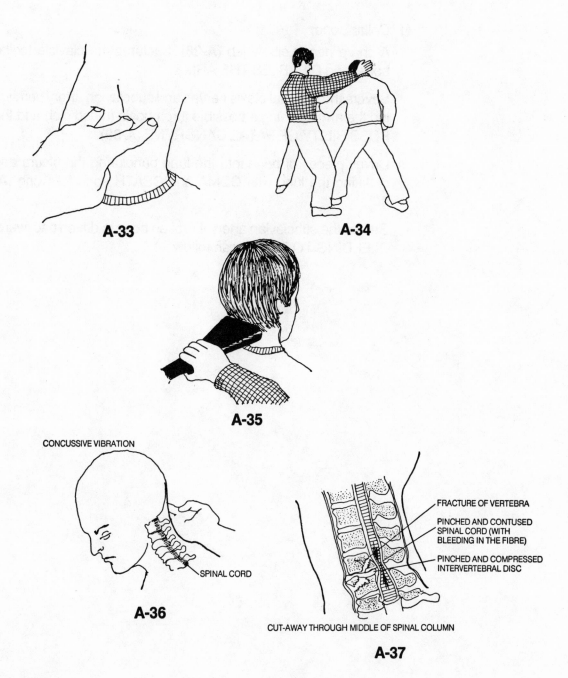

A-33

A-34

A-35

CONCUSSIVE VIBRATION

SPINAL CORD

A-36

FRACTURE OF VERTEBRA

PINCHED AND CONTUSED
SPINAL CORD (WITH
BLEEDING IN THE FIBRE)

PINCHED AND COMPRESSED
INTERVERTEBRAL DISC

CUT-AWAY THROUGH MIDDLE OF SPINAL COLUMN

A-37

VITAL AREAS OF THE NECK AND THROAT — *con't.:*

4) Collar Bone:

A sharp heavy elbow jab (**A-38**): fractures the clavicle (collar bone) and DISABLES THE ARM.

Severs the brachial plexis nerves and subclavian artery paralyzing the arm, causing a possible thrombosis (blood clot) and the POSSIBILITY OF FATAL GANGRENE (**A-39**).

Drives pieces of bone into the lung puncturing the pleura and deflating the lung with COMA and DEATH soon following (**A-40**).

Severs the subclavian artery if broken bone is driven backward; BLEEDING TO DEATH can follow.

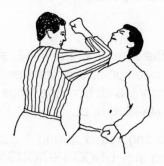

A-38

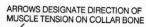
ARROWS DESIGNATE DIRECTION OF
MUSCLE TENSION ON COLLAR BONE

BRANCHIAL NERVE PLEXUS

CUT OFF BLOOD SUPPLY AND PINCHED
NERVE FROM FRACTURED COLLAR BONE

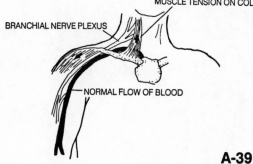
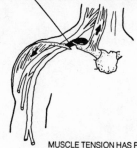

NORMAL FLOW OF BLOOD

A-39

MUSCLE TENSION HAS PULLED COLLAR
BONE DOWN ACROSS THE NERVES AND
ARTERY OF THE ARM

TEAR IN PLEUREA FROM FRACTURED COLLAR BONE

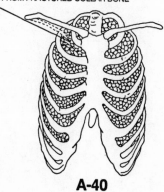

A-40

VITAL AREAS OF THE TORSO (A-41)

1) Diaphragm:

   A hammer-fist blow to the sternal angle **(A-42)** about 2 inches below the throat at the weak point over the heart, lungs, bronchus and thoracic nerve forces air from the lungs and results in UNCONSCIOUSNESS **(A-43 a, b, c)**.

   Fractures the ribs, irritating the diaphragm causing shallow breathing, painful hiccuping, UNCONSCIOUSNESS, COMA and DEATH **(A-44)**.

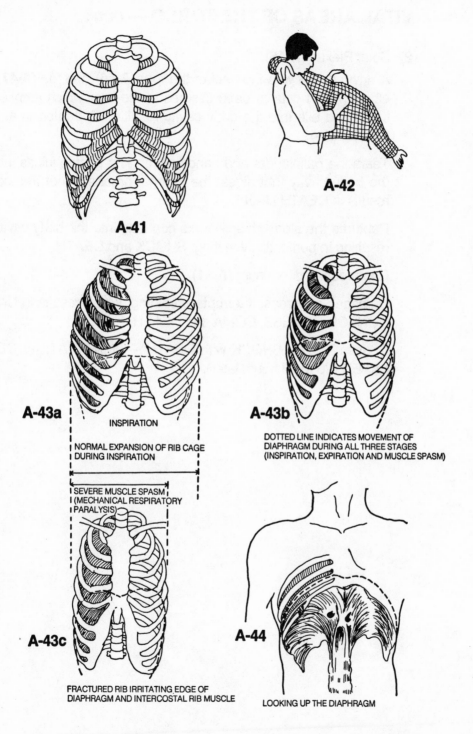

A-41

A-42

A-43a

INSPIRATION

NORMAL EXPANSION OF RIB CAGE
DURING INSPIRATION

SEVERE MUSCLE SPASM
(MECHANICAL RESPIRATORY
PARALYSIS)

A-43c

FRACTURED RIB IRRITATING EDGE OF
DIAPHRAGM AND INTERCOSTAL RIB MUSCLE

A-43b

DOTTED LINE INDICATES MOVEMENT OF
DIAPHRAGM DURING ALL THREE STAGES
(INSPIRATION, EXPIRATION AND MUSCLE SPASM)

A-44

LOOKING UP THE DIAPHRAGM

VITAL AREAS OF THE TORSO — *con't.:*

2) Solar Plexus (**A-45**):

A driving blow with the heel of the foot (**A-46**), the toe (**A-47**), elbow (**A-48**) causes deep fissures in the liver which empties blood and bile into the body cavity resulting in peritonitis and DEATH (**A-49**).

Tears the gallbladder and pancreas, spilling gastric juices into the body cavity that digest the internal organs; if not treated, results in DEATH (**A-50**).

Ruptures the stomach spilling its contents into the body cavity resulting in peritonitis, vomiting, SHOCK and DEATH.

Ruptures the duodenum (**A-51**).

Damages pancreas, interrupts breathing, which results in UN-CONSCIOUSNESS, COMA and DEATH.

Causes TOTAL SHOCK with DEATH — IMMEDIATE or DE-LAYED (up to 48 hours later).

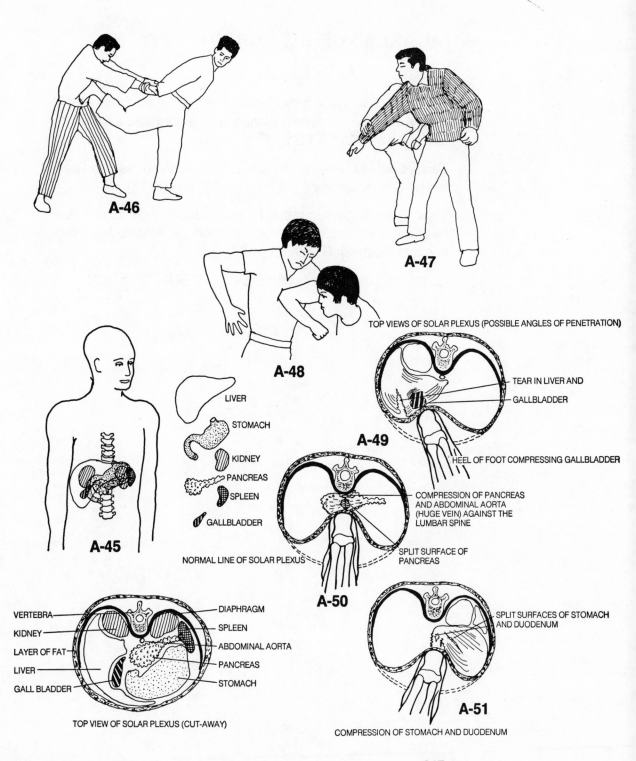

A-46

A-47

A-48

LIVER

STOMACH

KIDNEY

PANCREAS

SPLEEN

GALLBLADDER

A-45

TOP VIEWS OF SOLAR PLEXUS (POSSIBLE ANGLES OF PENETRATION)

TEAR IN LIVER AND

GALLBLADDER

A-49

HEEL OF FOOT COMPRESSING GALLBLADDER

COMPRESSION OF PANCREAS AND ABDOMINAL AORTA (HUGE VEIN) AGAINST THE LUMBAR SPINE

SPLIT SURFACE OF PANCREAS

NORMAL LINE OF SOLAR PLEXUS

A-50

VERTEBRA

KIDNEY

LAYER OF FAT

LIVER

GALL BLADDER

DIAPHRAGM

SPLEEN

ABDOMINAL AORTA

PANCREAS

STOMACH

TOP VIEW OF SOLAR PLEXUS (CUT-AWAY)

SPLIT SURFACES OF STOMACH AND DUODENUM

A-51

COMPRESSION OF STOMACH AND DUODENUM

VITAL AREAS OF THE TORSO — *con't.:*

3) Kidney:

Elbow drive to the kidney (**A-52**) or sharp object thrust (**A-53**) results in kidney rupture and massive hemorrhage followed by SHOCK and POSSIBLE DEATH (**A-54**).

Causes kidney lacerations from a broken rib and results in peritonitis, bloody urination, COMA and DEATH (**A-55**).

Urinary blockage can result from a glancing-type blow below last rib tearing the kidney from its moorings, followed by infection and POSSIBLE DEATH (**A-56**).

Collapsed lung possible with DEATH BY SUFFOCATION.

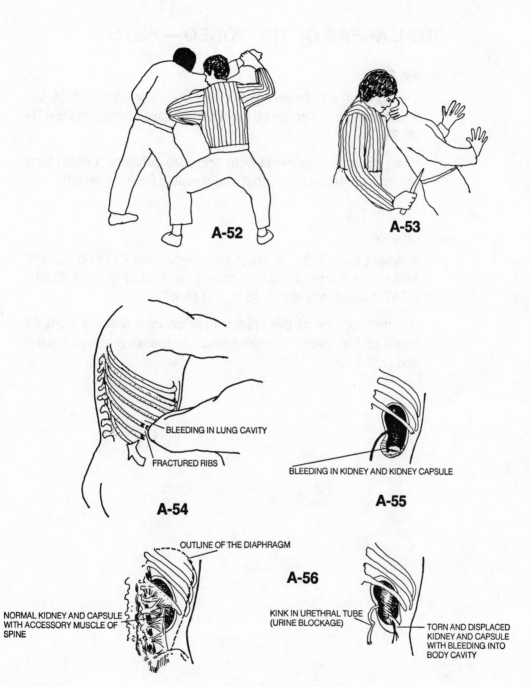

A-52

A-53

BLEEDING IN LUNG CAVITY

FRACTURED RIBS

A-54

BLEEDING IN KIDNEY AND KIDNEY CAPSULE

A-55

OUTLINE OF THE DIAPHRAGM

A-56

NORMAL KIDNEY AND CAPSULE
WITH ACCESSORY MUSCLE OF
SPINE

KINK IN URETHRAL TUBE
(URINE BLOCKAGE)

TORN AND DISPLACED
KIDNEY AND CAPSULE
WITH BLEEDING INTO
BODY CAVITY

VITAL AREAS OF THE TORSO — *con't.:*

4) Rib Cage:

Driving blow with heel or flat-of-foot (**A-57**) or knee kick (**A-58**) results in rib fracture and a possible collapsed lung and DEATH (**A-59**).

Heart spasms may result from pressure differential when lung collapses causing heart shift and possible DEATH (**A-60**).

5) Spleen:

A violent kick (**A-61**) or fist punch (**A-62**) results in rib fracture and spleen lacerations (rupture) with SLOW BUT SURE DEATH (generally within 48 hours) (**A-63**).

Delayed rupture of the spleen may occur anywhere from 24 hours to two years later and result in massive hemorrhaging and DEATH.

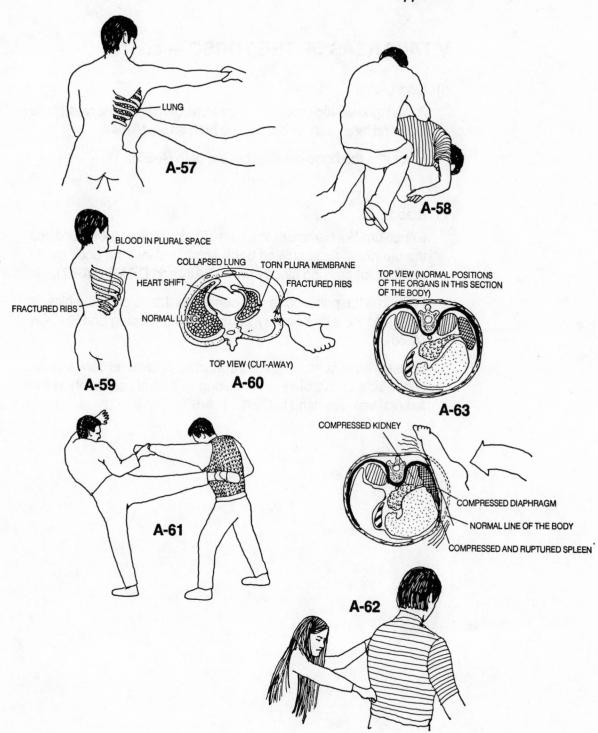

A-57

A-58

BLOOD IN PLURAL SPACE
FRACTURED RIBS
A-59

COLLAPSED LUNG   TORN PLURA MEMBRANE
HEART SHIFT   FRACTURED RIBS
NORMAL LUNG
TOP VIEW (CUT-AWAY)
A-60

TOP VIEW (NORMAL POSITIONS OF THE ORGANS IN THIS SECTION OF THE BODY)
A-63

A-61

COMPRESSED KIDNEY
COMPRESSED DIAPHRAGM
NORMAL LINE OF THE BODY
COMPRESSED AND RUPTURED SPLEEN
A-62

VITAL AREAS OF THE TORSO — *con't.:*

6) Coccyx:

   A driving knee kick causes nerve trunk damage to nerves of the hips and legs partially paralyzing both areas (**A-64**).

   Fractures the bone causing severe pain (**A-65**).

7) Bladder:

   Pendulum like hammer blow with the closed fist (**A-66**) ruptures the urinary bladder spilling urine and blood into the body cavity (peritonitis) causing bloody urine, PAIN and DEATH (**A-67**).

   Fractures the pubic bone and punctures the colon (if the blow is slightly to the left of center), causing hemorrhaging and SHOCK (**A-68**).

   Causes an inguinal or femoral hernia (if blow is low and on either side of the bladder) resulting in thrombosis (clot) in the femoral vein resulting in DEATH (**A-69**).

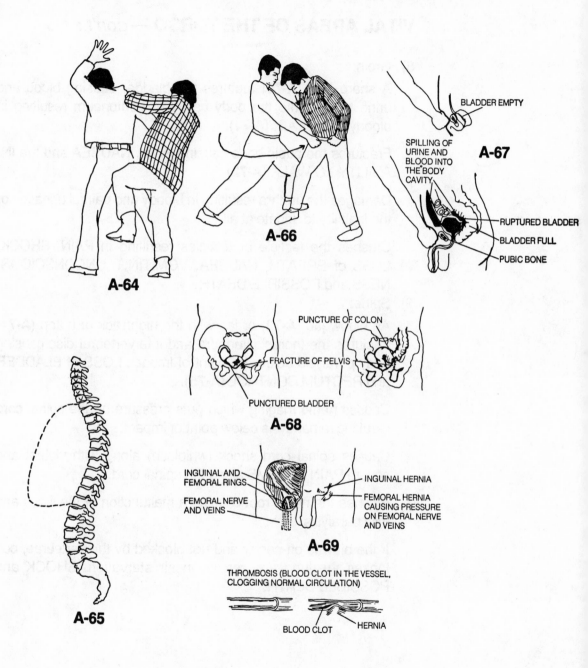

A-64

A-66

A-67

BLADDER EMPTY

SPILLING OF
URINE AND
BLOOD INTO
THE BODY
CAVITY

RUPTURED BLADDER

BLADDER FULL

PUBIC BONE

PUNCTURE OF COLON

FRACTURE OF PELVIS

PUNCTURED BLADDER

A-68

A-65

INGUINAL AND
FEMORAL RINGS

FEMORAL NERVE
AND VEINS

INGUINAL HERNIA

FEMORAL HERNIA
CAUSING PRESSURE
ON FEMORAL NERVE
AND VEINS

A-69

THROMBOSIS (BLOOD CLOT IN THE VESSEL,
CLOGGING NORMAL CIRCULATION)

BLOOD CLOT

HERNIA

VITAL AREAS OF THE TORSO — *con't.:*

8) Groin:

A sharp kick (**A-70**) ruptures the bladder causing blood and urine to flow into the body cavity or peritoneum resulting in bloody urine, PAIN (**A-71**).

Fractures the pubic bone causing PAIN, NAUSEA and the IN-ABILITY TO WALK (**A-72**).

Damages the urethra resulting in bloody and painful urination or the inability to urinate at all.

Crushes the testicle or testicles resulting in PAIN, SHOCK, LOSS of BREATH, NAUSEA, VOMITING, UNCONSCIOUS-NESS and POSSIBLE DEATH.

9) Spine:

An elbow jab (**A-73**) or jab with the nightstick or baton (**A-74**) fractures the thoracic vertebra and intervertebral disc causing body paralysis below the point of impact, LOSS of BLADDER and RECTUM CONTROL (**A-75**).

Causes hemorrhaging which puts pressure on the spinal cord resulting in paralysis below point of impact.

Causes spinal cord shock (whiplash) along with violent and severe PAIN SPASMS along the spinal cord.

Pinches the nerve root causing a malfunction of the limbs and mild paralysis.

If the blow is off-center and not blocked by the vertebrae, collapses the lung and results in air starvation, SHOCK and POSSIBLE DEATH.

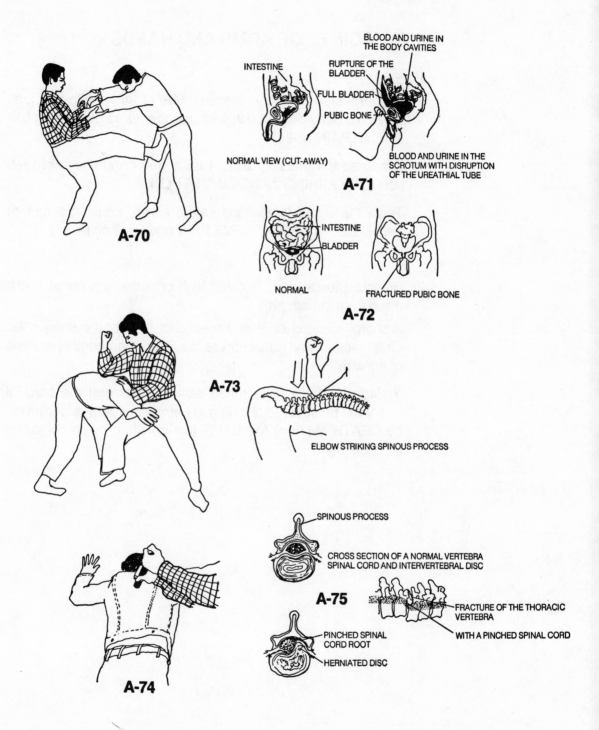

A-70

A-71

NORMAL VIEW (CUT-AWAY)

INTESTINE

RUPTURE OF THE BLADDER

FULL BLADDER

PUBIC BONE

BLOOD AND URINE IN THE BODY CAVITIES

BLOOD AND URINE IN THE SCROTUM WITH DISRUPTION OF THE UREATHIAL TUBE

A-72

INTESTINE

BLADDER

NORMAL

FRACTURED PUBIC BONE

A-73

ELBOW STRIKING SPINOUS PROCESS

A-74

A-75

SPINOUS PROCESS

CROSS SECTION OF A NORMAL VERTEBRA SPINAL CORD AND INTERVERTEBRAL DISC

PINCHED SPINAL CORD ROOT

HERNIATED DISC

FRACTURE OF THE THORACIC VERTEBRA

WITH A PINCHED SPINAL CORD

VITAL POINTS OF ARMS AND HANDS (A-76)

1) Elbow:

A sharp blow with the forearm (**A-77**) strike-with-the-hand (**A-78**) or body drop (**A-79**) fractures the humorus causing EXTREME PAIN (**A-80**).

Damages the brachial artery resulting in gangrene within 4-6 hours REQUIRING ARM AMPUTATION.

Tears the bursa (lubricating sac in elbow) causing a rupture (tennis elbow) and EXTREME PAIN and swelling (**A-81**).

2) Brachial plexus injury (located high on inner arm about 1 inch down from the armpit):

A sharp, clean chop with the edge of the hand damages the ulnar, median and radial nerves resulting in temporary paralysis of the arm.

If slashed with a knife these same nerves and the brachial artery will be severed resulting in permanent paralysis followed by DEATH WITHIN MINUTES (unless bleeding is contained immediately).

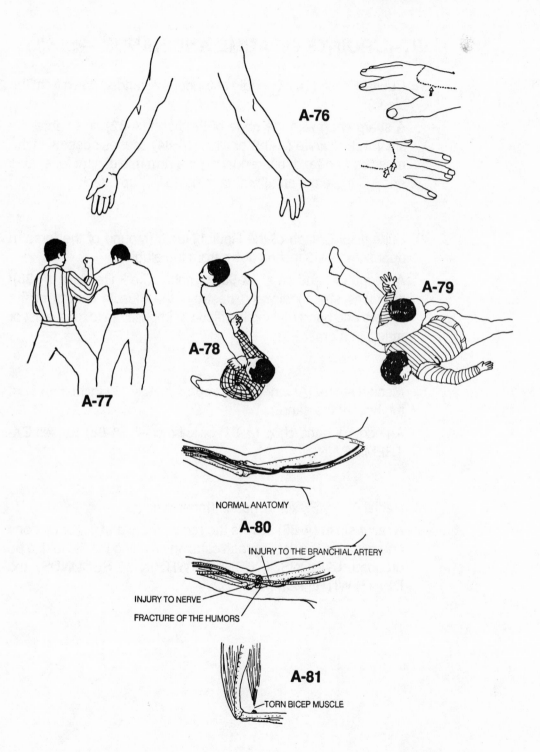

A-76

A-77

A-78

A-79

NORMAL ANATOMY

A-80

INJURY TO THE BRANCHIAL ARTERY

INJURY TO NERVE

FRACTURE OF THE HUMORS

A-81

TORN BICEP MUSCLE

VITAL POINTS OF ARMS AND HANDS — *con't.:*

3) Cubital Fossa (Thick bundle of tendons extended down from the bicep):

   A sharp chop with the edge of the hand (**A-82**) or a sabre-like slash with a knife (**A-83**) or razor (**A-84**) causes spasms in the muscles and tendons, rendering the arm useless, at least long enough to permit an alternate lethal follow-up attack.

4) Superficial Branch of the Radial Nerve (Mound of the forearm approximately 3 inches down from the elbow):

   An edge of hand chop (**A-85**) or sabre like knife slash (**A-86**)/ produces sharp pain and destroys the muscle control of the fingers and hand making it difficult or impossible to form a fist or maintain a grasp.

5) Median Nerve (At inner wrist approximately 1½ inches up from the heel of the hand):

   An edge of hand chop (**A-87**) or knife slash (**A-88**) causes EXTREME PAIN.

6) Radial Artery/Flexor Tendons (Inner Wrist):

   A razor slash (**A-88**) severs the radial artery and flexor tendons and releases the fist or grasp causing anything that is held to be dropped, UNCONSCIOUSNESS WITHIN 30 SECONDS, and DEATH WITHIN 2 MINUTES.

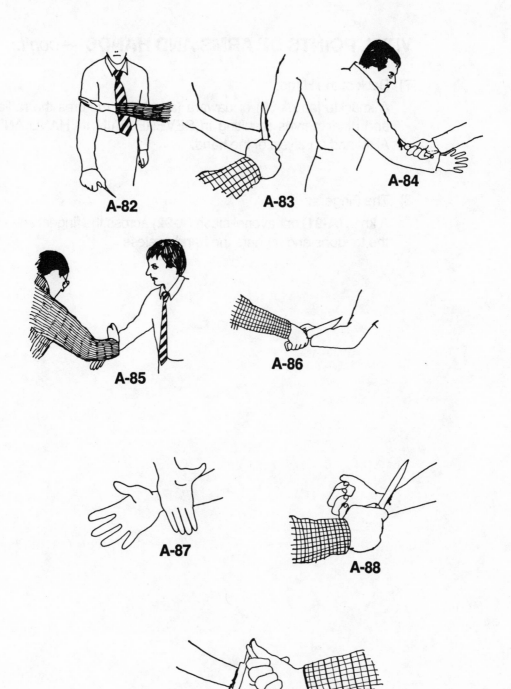

A-82

A-83

A-84

A-85

A-86

A-87

A-88

VITAL POINTS OF ARMS AND HANDS — *con't.:*

7) Back of the Hand:

A knuckle jab (**A-89**) or Jawara jab (**A-90**) ruptures the radial and ulnar nerves resulting in SEVERE PAIN IN HAND AND ARM and paralysis of the hand.

8) The Fingers:

A knife (**A-91**) or bayonet slash (**A-92**) across the fingers severs the tendons and renders the hand useless.

A-89

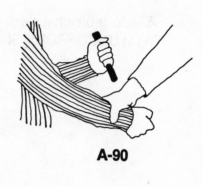

A-90

A-91

A-92

VITAL POINTS OF THE LEGS AND FEET (A-93)

1) Inguinal Region (Inside front upper thigh at testicles level):

   A sharp thumb or Jawara stick gouge (**A-94**) causes extreme pain.

   A knife or bayonet slash (**A-95**) severs the femoral artery resulting in UNCONSCIOUSNESS and DEATH WITHIN MINUTES.

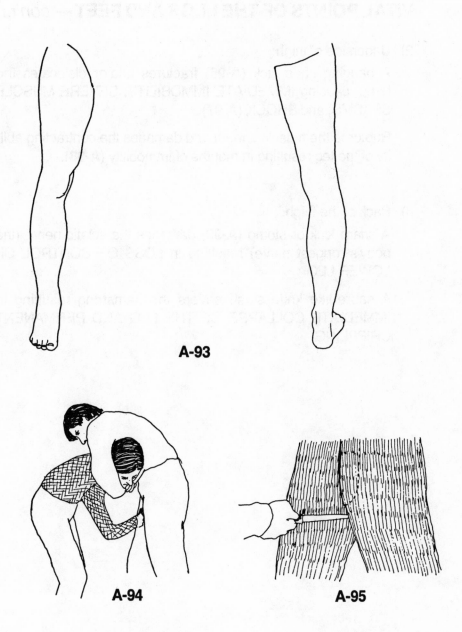

A-93

A-94

A-95

VITAL POINTS OF THE LEGS AND FEET — *con't.:*

2) Underside of thigh:

A banging knee kick (**A-96**) fractures and/or dislocates the femur causing IMMEDIATE IMMOBILITY, SEVERE MUSCLE SPASMS, and SHOCK (**A-97**).

Ruptures the muscle sheath and damages the contracting ability of the leg resulting in months of immobility (**A-98**).

3) Back of the thigh:

A sharp kick or stomp (**A-99**) damages the sciatic nerve (the body's longest nerve) resulting in LOSS OF CONTROL OF LOWER LEG.

A sabre-like knife slash severs the hamstring resulting in IMMEDIATE COLLAPSE OF THE LEG AND PERMANENT CRIPPLING.

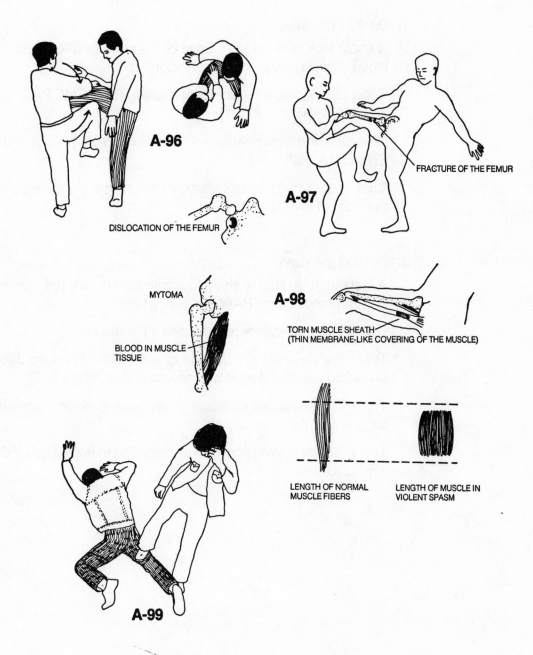

A-96

DISLOCATION OF THE FEMUR

A-97

FRACTURE OF THE FEMUR

MYTOMA

BLOOD IN MUSCLE
TISSUE

A-98

TORN MUSCLE SHEATH
(THIN MEMBRANE-LIKE COVERING OF THE MUSCLE)

LENGTH OF NORMAL
MUSCLE FIBERS

LENGTH OF MUSCLE IN
VIOLENT SPASM

A-99

VITAL POINTS OF THE LEGS AND FEET — *con't.:*

4) Back of the knee:

A sharp kick with the knife edge of the shoe (**A-100**) tears the blood vessels and produces a hemotoma.

Tears the muscle (torn kneecap) causing EXTREME PAIN and HELPLESSNESS. (**A-101**).

Dislocates the knee resulting in EXTREME PAIN, NAUSEA and SHOCK (**A-102**).

Causes spasms in the tabialis nerve resulting in paralysis below the point of impact.

5) Front of the knee:

A foot thrust (**A-103**) or sharp kick with the heel (**A-104**) sprains the knee and causes PAIN and STIFFNESS.

Ruptures the blood vessels, causes a hematoma.

Tears the bursa (lubricating sac of knee joint), spills the fluids under the skin resulting in a large lumpy swelling (**A-105**).

Tears the semilunar cartilage (knee joint cushion) requiring surgery (**A-106**).

Tears ligaments (avulsion fracture) resulting in IMMOBILITY OF THE LEG.

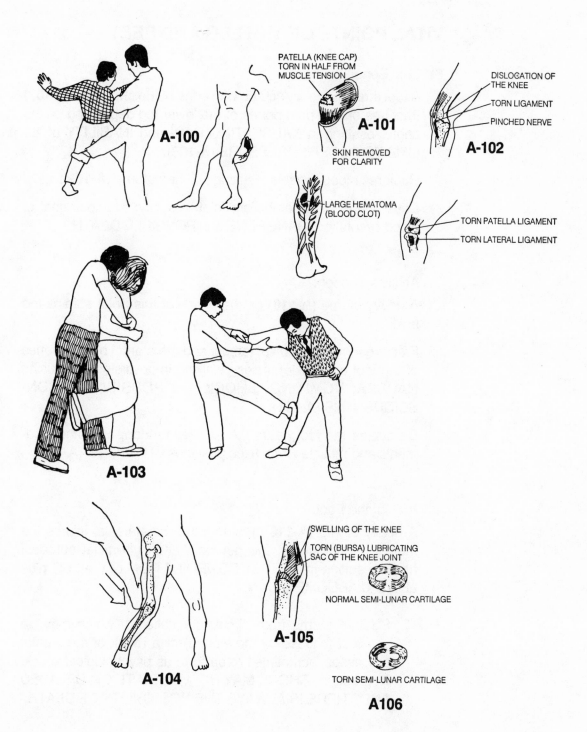

A-100

PATELLA (KNEE CAP)
TORN IN HALF FROM
MUSCLE TENSION

SKIN REMOVED
FOR CLARITY

A-101

DISLOCATION OF
THE KNEE

TORN LIGAMENT

PINCHED NERVE

A-102

LARGE HEMATOMA
(BLOOD CLOT)

TORN PATELLA LIGAMENT

TORN LATERAL LIGAMENT

A-103

A-104

SWELLING OF THE KNEE

TORN (BURSA) LUBRICATING
SAC OF THE KNEE JOINT

NORMAL SEMI-LUNAR CARTILAGE

A-105

TORN SEMI-LUNAR CARTILAGE

A106

VITAL POINTS OF THE LEG AND FEET — *con't.:*

6) Shin Bone:

A foot thrust or heavy scrape with edge of the shoe sole (**A-107**) fractures one or both bones of the lower leg depending on the angle resulting in NAUSEATING PAIN and INABILITY of the LIMB TO ACCEPT PRESSURE (**A-108**).

Ruptures blood vessels resulting in a hematoma (**A-109**).

Causes an arterial embolism (clot) resulting in impairment of blood circulation, GANGRENE and POSSIBLE DEATH.

7) Achilles Tendon:

A heavy stomp (**A-110**) or sharp kick at this point sprains the ankle.

Fractures the tibia, fibula, tarsus, and metatarsal bones (bones of the foot and ankle) making walking impossible and causing NAUSEA, VOMITING, SHOCK and POSSIBLE UNCON-SCIOUSNESS (**A-111**).

Dislocates the foot, tears the Achilles tendon, and other liga-ments and muscles from fixed positions CRIPPLING (**A-112**).

8) Arch of the Foot:

A heavy stomp (**A-113**) fractures the metatarsals, injures the medial plantar nerve, the peroneal and superficial peroneal nerve resulting in LOSS of COORDINATION of the LEG plus LEG and ABDOMEN PAIN.

NOTE: SHOCK stems from circulatory collapse which may be physical (caused by the wound) or a result of the mental processes, sometimes referred to as psychological shock. Regardless, SHOCK MAY BE IMMEDIATE OR DELAYED AND THERE IS ALWAYS THE POSSIBILITY OF DEATH.

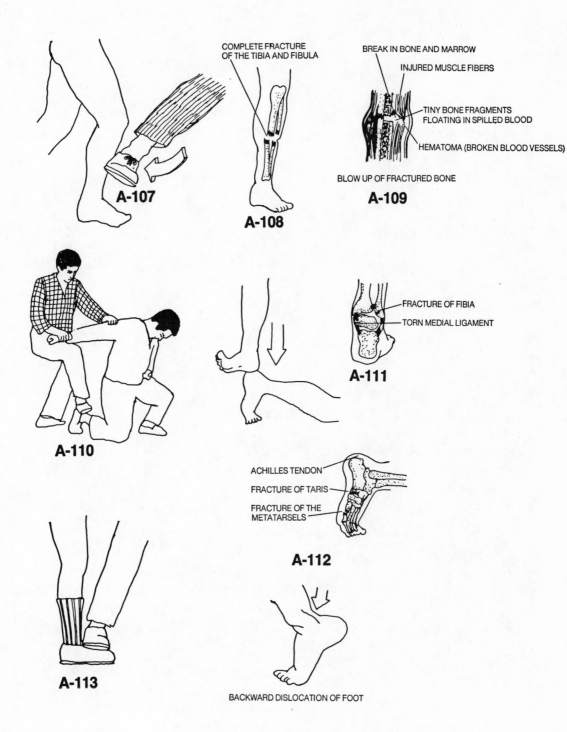

A-107

COMPLETE FRACTURE
OF THE TIBIA AND FIBULA

A-108

BREAK IN BONE AND MARROW

INJURED MUSCLE FIBERS

TINY BONE FRAGMENTS
FLOATING IN SPILLED BLOOD

HEMATOMA (BROKEN BLOOD VESSELS)

BLOW UP OF FRACTURED BONE

A-109

A-110

FRACTURE OF FIBIA

TORN MEDIAL LIGAMENT

A-111

ACHILLES TENDON

FRACTURE OF TARIS

FRACTURE OF THE
METATARSELS

A-112

A-113

BACKWARD DISLOCATION OF FOOT

239